Fighter Pilots of World War II

Robert Jackson

Fighter Pilots of World War II

St. Martin's Press

New York

Contents

Introduction 7
1 Paddy Finucane—the Leader 11
2 Frank Carey—Top Scorer? 21
3 'Johnnie' Johnson—the Hunter 31
4 Pattle—the Forgotten Hero 42
5 Richard Stevens—the Lonely Warrior 52
6 George Beurling—Malta Defender 59
7 Robert S. Johnson—Thunderbolt Pilot 70
8 Charles H. MacDonald—Lightning over Leyte 80
9 Adolf Galland—Fighter General 89
10 Erich Hartmann—Ace of Aces 100
11 Werner Mölders—the Veteran 112
12 Jochen Marseille—Eagle of the Desert 120
13 Saburo Sakai—Ace of the Rising Sun 130
14 Ivan Kozhedub—Russia's Top Scorer 145

Introduction

To select fourteen fighter pilots from the hundreds who fought with distinction on all sides during World War II has been a difficult, not to say impertinent task. In the end, as representative of all the others, I selected those who, to my mind, showed certain individual characteristics that seemed to set them apart.

Here, then, are the fourteen:

Paddy Finucane, one of the greatest and youngest leaders of men to rise to fame in the Royal Air Force;

Frank Carey, the modest Cockney ace whose battles in three campaigns were always fought against great odds;

'Johnnie' Johnson, who stalked his victims—all of them single-engined fighters—with cold, calculating skill;

'Pat' Pattle, probably the RAF's top-scoring pilot, eclipsed in the disaster that overwhelmed Greece in 1941;

Richard Stevens, a hunter without mercy in the night sky, whose family died under German bombs;

George Beurling, the rebel, whose first love was air combat;

Bob Johnson, Thunderbolt pilot, who helped to pioneer long-range fighter missions to the heart of Germany;

Charles MacDonald, whose fighter group took the war to the Japanese in the Pacific;

Adolf Galland, Fighter General, whose greatest battles were on the ground—against his superiors;

Erich Hartmann, ace of aces with 352 victories, all of them on the eastern front;

Werner Mölders, the veteran, beloved by all who served under him;

Jochen Marseille, chivalrous and flamboyant, who brought the *elan* of a bygone era to air warfare;

Saburo Sakai, Japan's leading surviving ace, who saw the Pacific air war from first to last;

Ivan Kozhedub, the peasant's son who fought his way from the Caucasus to the skies over Berlin.

'Choose as your inspiration a man who has done well, and follow his example all your life.'

Ivan Kozhedub—Fighter Pilot.

1 Paddy Finucane— the Leader

It was always easy to tell when the Spitfires had been in action. Instead of the compact Wing formation in which they had set out across the Channel they came straggling back to base in twos and threes, the slipstream whistling shrilly past the open ports in their wings through which spent 20-mm shell cases had been ejected.

That was how it was on the morning of 15 July 1942, when the Spitfires of the Hornchurch Wing came arcing down to land at their Essex airfield. As each aircraft taxied round to its dispersal it was seized by its ground crew, who inspected it lovingly for signs of tell-tale gashes in wings and fuselage as the tired pilot humped his parachute from the cockpit.

This morning, one crew waited in vain. They still waited, even when the news swept round Hornchurch like wildfire. Paddy Finucane was missing. Shot down into the Channel by a lone machine-gun on the enemy coast. Other pilots had seen him go down, his Spitfire sinking like a stone. There was no hope.

The word was received with incredulity. Paddy Finucane, a Wing Commander at the age of twenty-one with thirty-two confirmed victories to his credit, a man who had led a charmed life during his two years of operational flying—shot down in the end not by the Luftwaffe, but by a lucky burst from a machine-gun on the ground.

Brendan Finucane was born in Dublin in October 1920 of

an Irish father and English mother, the eldest of five children. His family was devoutly Catholic and he was educated at O'Connell's Irish Christian Brothers School until he was sixteen, when the Finucanes moved to Richmond in Surrey.

Soon after settling into his new home Paddy got a job as a clerk in a London accountant's office. He did not dislike his work; in fact he had a talent for working with figures, and during his RAF career he often said that he would like to go back to accounting after the war. Nevertheless, flying was in his blood; it was something he had to get out of his system, and as soon as he reached the minimum age of seventeen and a half in May 1938 he applied to join the RAF. He was quickly accepted for aircrew training, and almost exactly a year later he was posted to his first operational squadron.

His first sortie, early in June 1940, was a squadron patrol over the French coast, from which the remnants of the British Expeditionary Force were still being evacuated. In those days Fighter Command adhered strictly to rigid pre-war-style formations, and on this first trip Paddy was so preoccupied with keeping station that he had no time to scan the surrounding sky. Later, he learned that the squadron's presence had driven off a large formation of enemy aircraft, but he confessed that he had not seen them.

Combat experience, however, was to come rapidly. In July 1940 Paddy was posted to No. 65 Squadron at Hornchurch; the Germans were bombing convoys in the English Channel and 65's Spitfires were airborne almost continuously from Hornchurch and the advanced airfields at Manston and Rochford. During the next few days the young Irishman took part in several skirmishes, but it was not until 12 August that he got a chance to shoot down his first enemy aircraft.

Early that morning, the Battle of Britain began in earnest with an all-out blitz by the Luftwaffe on the RAF's front-line fighter airfields and the vital south coast radar stations. The radar reported a large force of hostile aircraft approaching the coast between Dover and Deal, and Finucane—who had been on readiness at Manston—took off with eleven other pilots to intercept them.

A few minutes later they sighted the enemy—twenty-plus Messerschmitt 109s—and split up into sections to attack. Paddy was flying in the Green 3 position, and as the battle was joined he saw a 109 shoot past him and fasten itself on the tail of his No. 2. He opened fire and the 109 sheered off, but then he in turn was attacked by two more enemy fighters and only managed to shake them off after a series of violent evasive manoeuvres. The danger over for the time being, he looked round and found himself alone in the sky. That was often the way in air combat; one moment a pilot would be surrounded by a whirling mass of fighters, the next he would have the sky to himself.

He climbed to 20,000 feet and scanned the horizon. Then, tilting a wing and looking down, he saw a dozen 109s in loose formation, heading out over the Channel. He was in a perfect position for an attack; a quick glance to the rear to make sure that nothing was on his tail and then he dived with the throttle wide open, closing on the rearmost aircraft. He opened fire at 250 yards and kept his thumb on the firing button until the last possible moment, half-rolling and diving away over the coast. Behind him, his victim went down in a vertical dive, dragging a thick column of smoke, and plunged into the sea.

He landed at Manston a few minutes later, tired and dripping with sweat. He had been airborne for just over an hour. There was to be no respite; just as the ground crews finished refuelling and rearming the Spitfires there came a new alert as a force of enemy bombers was reported approaching the airfield. The Spitfire pilots raced for their aircraft and were in the process of taking off when the enemy—twin-engined Messerschmitt 110s—swept overhead like a whirlwind, each releasing a pair of 1,000-pound bombs. Within minutes Manston was an inferno, but miraculously few of 65 Squadron's Spitfires suffered damage. In ones and twos the fighters climbed hard through the smoke that billowed over the airfield, looking for the 110s, but the German aircraft were well away by this time. Nevertheless the Spitfires stayed in the air, looking for action, and it was not long before they found it. The Luftwaffe seemed to be everywhere, and at 15,000 feet the Spitfires encountered fifteen Messerschmitt 109s. In the ensuing dogfight Paddy saw his bullets strike home on one enemy fighter, which he claimed as damaged.

There were to be no more victories for Paddy for several months. On 28 August No. 65 Squadron was sent to Turnhouse in Scotland, for a rest, and by the time it came south again the great air battles were over. In November 1940 the squadron was based at Tangmere, but the Germans had now switched to the night offensive against Britain's cities and during the winter months the Spitfire pilots saw little action. Paddy Finucane's next opportunity to score came on 4 January 1941, when he sighted a Messerschmitt 110 while on patrol over Selsey Bill. The German tried to escape by diving for cover in a thin layer of cloud, but Finucane overhauled him rapidly and opened fire at a range of three hundred yards, closing right in to twenty-five yards before breaking off. His bullets shattered the 110's cockpit and killed the rear gunner, after which the enemy pilot went into a series of desperate steep turns in an effort to get away. It was no use; Finucane made two more firing-passes and the 110 went down into the sea, disintegrating as it fell.

His next victim was a Junkers 88 bomber, which he shared with another pilot on 19 January. During this encounter his Spitfire was damaged, but he managed to reach base safely. A week later he destroyed a Messerschmitt 109, and claimed another aircraft of this type on 15 April.

It was his last kill with 65 Squadron. Soon afterwards he was posted as a flight commander to No. 452 Squadron, Royal Australian Air Force, which was then forming at Kirton Lindsey under the command of Squadron Leader R. G. Dutton, DFC. It was the first Australian fighter squadron in Europe, and was to achieve an impressive record before the end of hostilities. During the nine months it operated from Britain before being sent overseas, its pilots claimed sixty-two enemy aircraft destroyed plus seven 'probables' and seventeen damaged.

Finucane's posting to the Squadron as 'A' Flight Commander was a wise choice. The Australians took to the young Irishman immediately; quietly spoken and wise beyond his years, possessing all the native charm of his race, he exuded a mysterious—almost hypnotic—quality of leadership that no one who came into contact with him could fail to appreciate. He was as ready as the next man to enjoy a party in the mess, but he drank sparingly and encouraged those under him to do the same. Sometimes, on evenings when an operation was scheduled for the following day, he would stand apart in the crowded mess bar, quietly smoking his pipe and lost in thought. Then he would tap out his tobacco ash and stroll on his way to bed. Not a word would be spoken—but within a couple of minutes the other pilots would follow his example. Much of his inner strength seemed to stem from his religion; he attended Mass whenever he had the chance to do so, and yet he was far from a religious man in the conventional—or at any rate dogmatic—sense of the word. It was an attitude for which the tough Australians sincerely respected him.

On 10 June 1941 the squadron, now fully operational, moved to Kenley in Surrey under a new CO, Squadron Leader Bungey. A couple of weeks later another new pilot joined the unit as 'B' Flight Commander: Flight Lieutenant Keith 'Bluey' Truscott. Bungey, Finucane and Truscott made a formidable team, and during the months that followed they brought No. 452 to a peak of fighting efficiency.

The squadron's first contact with the enemy was made during a cross-Channel sweep on 11 July 1941, when four-

teen Spitfires tangled with 109s in the Abbeville area. Paddy
Finucane shot one down, chalking up 452's first victory. It
was only the start; between the end of July and the end of
October Paddy destroyed eighteen more 109s, shared two
others, claimed two as probably destroyed and three damaged, an achievement that brought him a DSO and two Bars
to the DFC he had earned earlier in the year.

One of the most hectic days during this period was 16 August, soon after Bluey Truscott had joined the squadron.
The Australian had already destroyed a 109 on 9 August;
now, a week later, he and Finucane were leading their
Spitfires into action again, escorting a squadron of Blenheim
bombers in an attack on a target in France. It was Paddy's
second sortie that day; during the first he had scored another victory. As the Spitfires were crossing the coast on
their way home eight Messerschmitts suddenly dived on
them from high astern. The Spits turned to meet them, and
in a violent ten-minute dogfight six 109s were shot down—
two of them by Finucane and one by Truscott. The battle
ended well out over the Channel with both sides short of
fuel. All the Spitfires returned safely to base; the only damage was a single bullet hole in one of them.

During these battles Finucane proved himself to be a very
careful fighter; he would not risk the lives of his pilots unless
the odds were in their favour. He had the ability, too, to
remain icily calm in a crisis, and it saved his life on more
than one occasion.

Once, while on his way home from a sweep, he and his
wingman spotted a lone Spitfire being attacked by two 109s
over the Channel. There was another formation of
Messerschmitts higher up, but Finucane decided that he
had enough time to get the solitary Spitfire out of its tight
corner before the whole lot descended. 'We went along
down,' he said later, 'and each of us shot down one of the
Mes into the water. That brought me pretty low, and I was
just above the surface when I saw cannon shells splashing

into the water in a steady stream, so I could figure that one of the big bunch of Jerries had followed me down and was at the back of me. It is a very good position to be in a fight because you can judge the angle of fire by the splashes, and then you know where your man is. As the angle gets smaller, you can figure he's getting in line with you. Just before that happens, you give a quick turn. If he doesn't follow, you whip up behind him and there you are. I got him and went home, quite happy, with the other lad.'

By the end of October 1941 Paddy's personal score stood at twenty-two enemy aircraft destroyed, and Bluey Truscott was coming up fast behind him with thirteen. The names of the two pilots—who were firm friends—began to feature regularly in Air Ministry bulletins, and there was much speculation about whether Bluey would catch up with the Irishman. Circumstances, however, were to prevent the friendly rivalry from developing; in November Paddy broke an ankle while jumping over a low wall in the blackout and was grounded for some weeks.

In January 1942 Finucane, newly promoted to Squadron Leader, was posted to command No. 602 (City of Glasgow) Squadron, which was operating from Hornchurch, while Truscott was given command of 452 in place of Bungey, who went to Shoreham.

It was not long before Finucane was in the news again. On 20 February 1942, together with an Australian pilot named Flying Officer Richard Lewis, he was in the process of strafing an enemy ship near Dunkirk when the two Spitfires were subjected to a head-on attack by a pair of Focke-Wulf 190s. Seconds later, shell splinters wounded Paddy in the leg and thigh. He immediately called up Lewis, ordering him to head for home as fast as possible. Instead, Lewis took up station behind Finucane, guarding him like a watchdog as he limped out over the Channel. The 190s were still pressing home determined attacks and Lewis turned to face them six times, driving them off with well-aimed bursts; one of them went down in a shallow glide and ditched. Finucane himself turned to face the other, which soon broke off the fight.

Paddy was now desperately weak from loss of blood, but somehow he managed to nurse his Spitfire over the English coast. He landed safely, taxied in and switched off his engine—then passed out in the cockpit. Fortunately his injury was not too serious, and on 13 March he returned to operations with a flourish, destroying a Fw 190 and sharing a second while escorting medium bombers in an attack on a French marshalling yard.

A couple of days later, he visited 452 Squadron to say goodbye to Bluey Truscott and the others, who were being posted back to Australia as part of the RAAF's growing commitment against the Japanese. It was a poignant moment, for the squadron had established many heart-warming friendships during its months in England.

Paddy's score went on growing. On 27 March 1942, the Air Ministry Bulletin ran: 'This afternoon, squadrons of Fighter Command swept the Channel area from Le Havre to Dunkirk. Thirteen enemy aircraft were destroyed. Squadron Leader Finucane destroyed two in this engagement, bringing his total score to twenty-nine.'

During the next two months Finucane shot down three more Fw 190s, bringing his confirmed score to thirty-two. He summed up his success very simply; 'I have been blessed with a pair of good eyes and have learned to shoot straight. The first necessity in combat is to see the other chap before he sees you or before he gets the tactical advantage of you. The second is to hit him when you fire. You may not get another chance.'

On 27 June he was appointed Wing Commander Flying at Hornchurch. Three weeks later, on 15 July, he took off at the head of his Spitfires to carry out a large-scale sweep over France, shooting up enemy installations. On the homeward journey Paddy crossed the coast at low level near Le Touquet, his eyes turned skywards in search of prowling enemy fighters. He never saw the lone machine-gun on the dune below. A bullet shattered his Spitfire's vulnerable radiator, and within seconds his engine began to overheat badly.

He could have turned back and made a forced landing in France—but being taken prisoner was one of his greatest fears, and instead he pointed his fighter's nose out over the Channel. Over the R/T his companions heard him call: 'I shall have to get out of this. Hello, Wing Commander calling. I've had it. Am turning out.'

Ten miles out to sea his juddering engine finally let him down and he began to lose height. His wingman, Pilot Officer F. A. Aikman, drew alongside and saw Finucane pull off his helmet. The crippled Spitfire continued to glide down, trailing a slender black ribbon. For the last time, they heard his voice: 'This is it, chaps.' As always the words were quiet and calm. The Spitfire hit the water tail-first and vanished under the surface, with hardly a ripple to mark its passing. Aikman circled overhead, waiting for Finucane to bob to the surface. But there was nothing; just a film of oil, spreading on the water.

He had been the nation's hero, and now the nation mourned him. More than three thousand people attended his Requiem Mass, held in Westminster Cathedral; the Mayor of Richmond in Surrey launched a nationwide appeal for a Finucane Memorial. Telegrams and letters of condolence reached Paddy's parents from all quarters: from squadrons, individuals, even a pair of leading Russian fighter pilots—and from Bluey Truscott.

Six months later, three days before Christmas, Finucane's father broadcast over the radio to Australia. His message ended: 'Especially do we remember and send our sincere wishes for a happy landing to Squadron Leader Bluey Truscott who, before he left this country, led the immortal band of fighter pilots who formed the first Australian Spitfire squadron . . .' And then, in Gaelic: 'God's blessing be with you.'

In March 1943, after adding three Japanese bombers to his score, Bluey Truscott was flying his Kittyhawk fighter on a practice interception detail against an Australian flying boat. After one run, his fighter swept beneath the larger aircraft; the location was just off the coast of New Guinea, near Port Moresby.

The flying boat crew waited for the fighter to reappear and make another dummy run. When it failed to do so, they circled in time to see the tell-tale oil slick that marked Truscott's grave. Like Paddy Finucane, the sea had claimed him.

2 Frank Carey—
Top Scorer?

It was 29 January 1942, 11.00 hours. For the past ten minutes the RAF ground personnel on the air base at Mingaladon, near Rangoon, had huddled in their slit trenches as
waves of Japanese aircraft swept overhead, unloading their
sticks of bombs on the airfield and targets around the
nearby city. Now, suddenly, the danger from bomb and bullet was forgotten and the airmen emerged from their shel-
ters into the open, faces upturned to watch a remarkable
duel that was taking place a few hundred feet above their
heads.

Round and round the airfield perimeter, as though on a
racing track, flew a Nakajima Ki.27 fighter, its single engine roaring under full power. A few yards behind, apparently attached to the tail of the enemy fighter by an
invisible thread, was a lone Hawker Hurricane, its
machine-guns hammering in short bursts. The watchers on
the ground saw pieces fall from the Japanese fighter and it
began to trail a thin stream of smoke. Expectantly, they
waited for it to plunge into the ground, but miraculously it
kept flying.

In the cockpit of the solitary Hurricane, Squadron Leader
Frank Carey was doing a lot of swearing. The squadron he
commanded, No. 135, had only recently arrived in Burma,
and this was his first chance to come to grips with the
enemy in the Far East. He was intent on turning the Ki.27
into the unit's first victim, but although he could see his bul-

lets ripping into the enemy's fuselage around the cockpit the nimble little Japanese fighter stubbornly refused to go down.

Then, abruptly, the Ki.27 wavered and altered course, entering a shallow dive towards a line of parked Blenheim bombers. It struck the ground in an enormous cloud of dust and smoke, pulverising one of the Blenheims, and disintegrated. Later, when RAF doctors examined the Japanese pilot's body, they found no fewer than twenty-seven bullets lodged in it. It was a miracle that the man had been able to remain in control of his aircraft for so long, and a grim indication of the courage and tenacity of the foe the Hurricane pilots of 135 Squadron were now facing.

At the age of thirty Frank Carey was considerably older than the average fighter pilot, and his career to date had been a good deal more varied than most. Born in Brixton, south-west London, on 7 May 1912, he was educated at the Belvedere School, Haywards Heath in Sussex, and a few days after leaving at the age of fifteen he signed on as an Aircraft Apprentice in the Royal Air Force. In 1927, after passing through the apprentice school at Halton, he was posted to the famous No. 43 'Fighting Cocks' Squadron as a rigger and fitter, in which trade he remained for the next three years. He then took an engineering course, at the end of which he applied for flying training and was accepted. In 1935 he completed his flying course at RAF Netheravon with high marks and was posted to his old unit, No. 43 Squadron at Tangmere, as a Sergeant Pilot.

Flying graceful little Hawker Fury biplane fighters he quickly made a name for himself as an aerobatic pilot, demonstrating his skill at the air pageants that were a regular feature of the carefree peacetime life of the RAF in the mid-1930s. The storm-clouds, however, were gathering on the horizon, and the RAF was belatedly striving to put its front-line squadrons on a more modern footing. In 1938 No. 43 became one of the first units to re-equip with Hawker Hurri-

canes, and a year later the outbreak of war found Carey
flying one of these machines in the squadron's 'A' Flight.

During the first weeks of the war the squadron was
mainly occupied in carrying out shipping patrols, a routine
that became increasingly boring as the winter of 1939-40
dragged on. Carey's first chance to fire his guns in anger
came on 29 January 1940, when—together with two other
pilots—he intercepted a Heinkel 111 ten miles east of Co-
quet Island. The running fight that followed was incon-
clusive, and although the Heinkel appeared to have been
damaged it succeeded in getting away.

At this time, enemy aircraft were becoming increasingly
active off the north-east coast, and to help counter this
threat No. 43 Squadron moved to Acklington, near Morpeth
in Northumberland, at the beginning of February. On 3
February Carey saw action again, when during a routine patrol east of the Tyne with another Hurricane he sighted a
Heinkel 111 about to attack a small coaster. Carey came in
from astern, opening fire at four hundred yards and continuing to fire down to a range of only twenty-five yards before
breaking off. His number two attacked in turn while Carey
circled for another run. The two Hurricanes made four firing
passes against the enemy bomber, which glided down and
ditched in the sea. Orbiting overhead, Carey saw the five
crew scramble clear; a few minutes later they were picked
up by a fishing boat.

A few days later, while leading a section of two Hurricanes, Carey caught another Heinkel over the North Sea
and shot it down in flames. At the end of February he was
awarded the Distinguished Flying Medal, and in March he
received a Commission, reporting to No. 3 Squadron as a
Pilot Officer a fortnight later. Early in May No. 3 Squadron
took its Hurricanes to France, and had scarcely had time to
settle in at Merville when the Germans launched their offensive in France and the Low Countries on 10 May 1940. That
first day of the invasion was a hectic one, with fierce air bat-

tles raging over Belgium and northern France. Early that morning, Carey was taking part in a squadron patrol when twenty enemy aircraft were sighted bombing Allied positions ten miles north-east of Lille. The Hurricanes ripped into the enemy formation and dogfights spread across the sky as individual pilots selected their targets.

Carey latched on to a Heinkel, firing short bursts from close range. His bullets found their mark in the bomber's engines, which began to stream smoke, and destroyed its hydraulic system, causing the undercarriage to come down. A moment later the Heinkel went into a spin and dived into the ground. Carey immediately climbed up and returned to the fight, claiming hits on three more aircraft before he was forced to return to base, out of ammunition.

On 12 and 13 May he shot down two Junkers 87s and claimed two more probably destroyed, and on 14 May he shot down a Dornier 17. The rear-gunner of this aircraft, however, continued to fire at Carey's Hurricane even when the bomber was going down in flames, hitting the fighter in the engine and wounding its pilot in the right leg. Although in pain and weakened by loss of blood Carey managed to make a successful forced landing near Grez-Doiceau, southeast of Brussels. As he scrambled from the cockpit of his wrecked fighter he saw a small party of motor-cycle troops bumping across the field towards him. The German advance had been extremely rapid and he had no way of knowing whether he was in enemy territory or not, so he drew his pistol and prepared to shoot it out. The soldiers however were Belgians, who took him to the nearby village and handed him over to a detachment of British sappers. They bandaged his leg and he hitched a lift into Brussels, where he was able to receive more thorough treatment.

Carey tried to telephone his squadron at Merville to tell them what had happened, but communications had broken down and he was unable to get through. In fact he was destined to see no further action with No. 3 Squadron. During the days that followed he was shuttled from one military hospital to another in the path of the German advance. He finally obtained a discharge and reported to No. 26 Aircraft Depot, where several other shot-down RAF pilots were also trying to locate their squadrons. After a day or two it became apparent that the position was completely hopeless, and they decided to try and reach England under their own steam. Scouting around for a suitable means of transport they found an elderly Bristol Bombay aircraft, amazingly still in an airworthy condition, at a nearby airstrip and obtained permission to fly it home. It was not until he arrived safely on the other side of the Channel that Carey found he had been posted missing, believed killed.

Shortly after his return he was posted back to No. 43 Squadron as a flight commander. By this time the Battle of France was almost over and the Luftwaffe was beginning to probe out across the Channel, its targets the coastal convoys. In the afternoon of 19 June 1940, Carey and his flight took off from Tangmere to patrol in the direction of the French coast. Over the Channel they spotted a formation of Messerschmitt 109s a few thousand feet higher up. The German pilots had seen the Hurricanes and came down to the attack, but Carey's flight broke expertly at the last moment and the enemy overshot. Carey turned on to the tail of the rearmost 109 and got in a lengthy deflection shot, hitting the enemy fighter in the fuselage. The 109 turned over on to its back and went down through a thin layer of cloud, with Carey following. He broke cloud in time to see the column of spray subsiding where the fighter had hit the water, and pieces of wreckage floating on the surface. Climbing back into the fight Carey fired several bursts at another 109 and saw his tracers striking home. The enemy fighter managed to get away and disappeared towards the French coast.

During July Carey added two more aircraft to his score: a Messerschmitt 110 on the 9th and a 109 on the 19th. Then, in August, the Battle of Britain began in earnest. On the

12th and 13th, the first two days of the heavy Luftwaffe attacks on the RAF airfields in the south of England, Carey claimed two Junkers 88s, and on the 16th he was involved in a fierce air battle over the south coast. His combat report describes the action:

I was leading 'A' Flight behind the leader of the squadron having taken off at 12.45 hours to patrol Selsey Bill at 11,000 ft. when I gave Tally Ho on sighting waves of Ju 87s. The leader ordered the squadron to attack one formation of 87s from the front and immediately on closing the leader of the enemy aircraft was hit by Squadron Leader and crew baled out.

I pulled my flight over to the left to attack the right hand formation as we met them. Almost as soon as I opened fire, the enemy aircraft's crew baled out and the machine crashed in the sea, just off Selsey Bill. I turned to continue my attack from the rear as enemy aircraft were completely broken up by frontal attack and several other waves behind them turned back out to sea immediately although we had not attacked them. I picked out one Ju 87 and fired two 2-second bursts at him and the enemy aircraft burst into flames on the port wing root.

I did not wait to see it crash as I turned to attack another. After one burst at the third enemy aircraft, two large pieces of metal broke off the port wing and the enemy aircraft seemed to stop abruptly and go into a dive but I did not see the machine crash as two other Ju 87s were turning on to my tail. I eventually picked on a fourth, but after firing two bursts and causing the engine to issue black smoke, the enemy aircraft turned out to sea and I ran out of ammunition. I noticed firing behind me and turned to see a pair of Me 109s behind me, one firing and the other apparently guarding his tail. After a few evasive actions enemy aircraft broke off and I returned to land and refuel and rearm at 13.40 hours.

Two days later, while leading 43 Squadron on patrol, Carey encountered another large formation of Ju 87s near Chichester. He shot down one Stuka, but his own aircraft was repeatedly hit by machine-gun fire and he was wounded in the right knee. He brought his Hurricane down for a successful forced landing near Pulborough, and spent the next couple of weeks recuperating in the Royal Sussex Hospital at Chichester.

By the time he was fit enough to return to operations in mid-September his squadron had been posted north for a rest, and RAF Fighter Command had shattered once and for all the Luftwaffe's hopes of gaining air superiority over the British Isles. Carey's score now stood at 18 enemy aircraft destroyed. In the space of six months he had risen from Sergeant Pilot to Squadron Leader and had been awarded the DFM, DFC and Bar.

At the end of 1940 Carey was posted to No. 52 Operational Training Unit at Debden, Essex, where he spent the next few months as an instructor. He then went to Northern Ireland to join No. 245 Squadron, but spent only a short time with this unit before being appointed commanding officer of the newly-formed No. 135 Squadron, which was working up to operational standard on Hurricanes. On 6 December 1941 this unit sailed for Rangoon to bolster the RAF's pitifully weak air defences in Burma. Twenty-four hours later, in the wake of their devastating attack on Pearl Harbor, the Japanese launched their offensives in the Pacific and South-East Asia.

On 12 February, shortly after his preliminary skirmishes with the Japanese Air Force, Carey was promoted to Wing Commander and placed in command of the two squadrons of Hurricanes which formed the RAF Fighter Wing at Mingaladon. Japanese air activity was increasing all the time, and on 23 February Carey intercepted and destroyed an enemy reconnaissance aircraft over Rangoon. On the 26th, in the course of three separate sorties, he shot down three Nakajima Ki.43 'Oscar' fighters, bringing his score in the Far East to five and his total score to twenty-three. Soon after this exploit he received a second Bar to his DFC.

The main task of the Mingaladon Wing was to cover the progressive withdrawal of the Allied forces, who were being pushed steadily back towards the Indian frontier by the relentless Japanese advance. For operational purposes the RAF Hurricanes, working in close co-operation with the P-40

Tomahawk fighters of the American Volunteer Group, whose veteran pilots had been fighting the Japanese in China for some considerable time before the attack on Pearl Harbor, were scattered over a number of makeshift airstrips in the Rangoon area. This reduced the risk of losses during enemy air attacks, but made it difficult to mount a sizeable force of fighters for either attack or defence at short notice.

This was the problem that faced Carey when, at the beginning of March, he received information that a large number of Japanese fighters and bombers were moving into the captured airfield at Moulmein, just across the Gulf of Martaban and close to the border with Thailand. Carey immediately mustered his eight remaining serviceable Hurricanes and ordered them to take off for a strike on the enemy field. Just as the RAF fighters were leaving their respective airstrips however, Japanese aircraft appeared overhead and it was not possible for the Hurricanes to make rendezvous with one another.

Carey accordingly set course for Moulmein accompanied by only two other Hurricanes. One of these got lost *en route;* Carey and the remaining pilot, Pilot Officer Underwood, pressed on and arrived over Moulmein to find that the intelligence report had been correct. The airfield was crammed with enemy fighters, many standing in neat rows while ground crews refuelled and rearmed them.

Carey selected two Oscars which were approaching to land, well committed with their wheels and flaps down. One short burst and the rearmost of the two fighters crashed on the end of the runway. Carey went after the other, which went into a steep turn just as the RAF pilot opened fire. It was a fatal mistake; the Jap's airspeed was too low. His wing tip hit the ground and he cartwheeled in a great arc, ploughing through a line of fighters and blowing up among the canvas hangars.

Carey raced across the airfield and pulled up steeply to look for Underwood, but there was no sign of him. By this time the Japanese were thoroughly aroused, and Carey found himself running the gauntlet of a swarm of enemy fighters. For five of the longest minutes in his life he jinked and twisted round the airfield; an Oscar made the mistake of turning steeply in front of him and he sent it down with one well-aimed burst. The Japanese fighters were getting in each other's way, and eventually Carey spotted an opening and headed for it at full throttle. The Japs chased him across the jungle for some distance, then gave up. Carey landed at Mingaladon with his aircraft riddled like a colander. Later, he learned that Underwood had been hit by flak and taken prisoner after baling out.

On 8 March the Japanese entered Rangoon, and it was no longer possible for the Allies to carry out an organized defence of Burma. The army now began the long retreat northwards along the Irrawaddy and Sittang Rivers, protected by the handful of P-40s and Hurricanes that remained. Operating from a series of rough strips hacked out of the jungle between Rangoon and Mandalay, these aircraft maintained air cover over the retreating forty-mile-long British convoy. By the end of March the battle for Burma had been lost, and the battered fighter squadrons withdrew to India to rest and re-equip.

In 1943, Carey's 135 Squadron was one of the RAF fighter units that returned to the fray in support of Wavell's offensive against the Japanese in the Arakan. By the middle of the year the allies had thirty-one fighter squadrons in the India-Burma Theatre—a far cry from the gloomy picture of a year earlier—and they rapidly gained uncontested air superiority over the enemy. In May 1943 135 Squadron was based at Chittagong, and it was here that Carey's final brush with the Japanese took place. A formation of enemy bombers tried to attack the airfield, but they were intercepted and driven off by Carey and one other pilot, Flying Officer R. Storey. During the ensuing fight, Carey at one stage found no fewer than six Oscar fighters on his tail. He roared across the jungle at low level, pulling up steeply at the last minute to avoid a hillside. One of his pursuers was not quick enough and crashed among the trees.

Carey's tour in the Far East was now at an end, and he returned to England to attend Gunnery School. After that he was posted back to India to form an Air Fighting Training Unit at Calcutta. In November 1944 he was promoted to Group Captain and went to Egypt to become commanding officer of No. 73 Operational Training Unit at Abu Suweir in the Canal Zone. The end of the war found him at the Central Fighter Establishment as Group Captain (Tactics).

With the shooting over, he reverted to the rank of Wing Commander and spent a year at the RAF Staff College, Camberley. In 1949 he took a jet conversion course on Vampires and became Wing Commander Flying at Gutersloh, in Germany. Promoted once more to Group Captain he held a number of other appointments within RAF Fighter Command before joining the UK Joint Services Liaison Staff as Air Adviser to the High Commissioner in Australia, a post he held from 1958 to 1960. On his retirement from the RAF he decided to stay in Australia and became a senior representative for Rolls-Royce Ltd in Canberra.

According to official records, Frank Carey ended World War II with a score of twenty-eight enemy aircraft destroyed. He himself believes it to be somewhat higher. The problem was that although he scored several kills during the long retreat from Burma in 1942, these could not be confirmed officially as his unit's records were lost or destroyed. Some sources claim that his total score could be as high as fifty. If that is so, it would make Frank Carey the top-scoring British Commonwealth or American fighter pilot to emerge from the Second World War. The exact figure, however, will never be known.

3 'Johnnie' Johnson— the Hunter

A great many differing factors go into the makeup of a successful fighter pilot. Skill and reflex are only two of the essentials. Equally as important in forming the overall picture, or so most wartime fighter 'aces' would claim, are the prevailing circumstances at the time air combat takes place— and that indefinable ingredient known loosely as luck.

Most of the RAF's leading fighter pilots achieved their heaviest scores during the savage fighting in the Battles of France and Britain. Later in the war, the American Mustang, Lightning and Thunderbolt pilots who escorted the great formations of B-17s and B-24s to the heart of Germany fought from a position of considerable superiority, both technical and numerical. The Pacific Theatre was a totally different environment, becoming a vast graveyard of Japanese aircraft; nowhere else, from 1943 onwards, did the Allied fighters destroy so many enemy machines in such a comparatively short time.

Among all the Allied fighter pilots of the Second World War, one man stands out as a classic example of the picture evoked by the term 'fighter pilot'; a man whose victories were achieved in the manner of the hunter, stalking and engaging his prey in cold, ruthless single combat. He destroyed thirty-eight enemy aircraft, all of them single-engined fighters. His name is James Edgar Johnson, and he is officially the RAF's top-scoring pilot of World War II.

Born at Melton Mowbray, the son of a police inspector,

'Johnnie' Johnson was educated at Loughborough School and in 1938, at the age of twenty-two, qualified as a civil engineer in Nottingham. Keen on flying since his boyhood, he applied to join an Auxiliary Air Force squadron as a trainee pilot, but although he was already taking flying tuition privately he was not accepted. He then tried to join the RAF Volunteer Reserve, in which some of his friends were already serving, but found that there were no vacancies at the VR training schools—so he enlisted in the Leicestershire Yeomanry, a mounted Territorial unit.

Returning home from Annual Camp with the Yeomanry in 1939, he found a letter from the Air Ministry awaiting him. It had been decided to expand the RAFVR, and there were now vacancies. Forty-eight hours later, he reported to the VR headquarters in London for interview and medical examination, and that same day—bewildered by the speed of it all—he was sworn in as a Sergeant Pilot (Under Training).

He learned to fly on Tiger Moths at Stapleford Tawney and Cambridge, finally completing his course as a qualified pilot in the spring of 1940, just as the Germans launched their Blitzkrieg in western Europe. After an advanced flying course he flew a Spitfire for the first time at Hawarden, an Operational Training Unit, and at the end of August he was ordered to report to his first squadron—No. 19, at Duxford, as a newly-commissioned Pilot Officer.

Any hopes Johnson entertained of coming to speedy grips with the enemy were soon shattered. The squadron was fully committed to the great air battle raging over southern England, and there was no time to initiate new and inexperienced pilots into combat. After kicking his heels in frustration around the airfield for several days, watching the Spitfires take off on one sortie after another, he was posted to No. 616 Squadron at Coltishall. This unit had just been pulled out of the line for a rest, and would have time to train replacements.

Soon after his arrival the squadron moved to Kirton Lindsey, in Lincolnshire, where the days were spent in air fighting practice. After a week or two, Johnson developed a severe pain in his right shoulder: the result of an old injury sustained while playing rugby, a broken collar bone that had not knit properly. He went into hospital to have the bone reset, and it was not until December 1940 that he rejoined his unit.

In February 1941 No. 616 moved south to Tangmere, where it formed part of a wing of three squadrons commanded by Douglas Bader, the legless pilot whose name was already legendary. During March and April Johnson took part in several cross-Channel 'sweeps' with the Tangmere Wing, but although he sighted enemy fighters he was not able to engage them. His chance finally came in May 1941 when, during a sweep over Gravelines, the Tangmere Wing was 'bounced' by Messerschmitt 109s and a fierce air battle developed. A 109 appeared in a shallow dive in front of Johnson, who hit him at close range with fire from the Spitfire's eight machine-guns. The enemy fighter went over on its back and the pilot baled out. Johnnie returned home, elated, to find that his 'kill' had been seen and confirmed by several other pilots.

During the weeks that followed the Tangmere Wing carried out many sorties over enemy-occupied France, usually acting as escort to RAF medium bomber squadrons. Johnson usually flew as Bader's No. 2, and in those summer months he learned much about the science of air fighting from the more experienced pilot. By the autumn of 1941—following a spell of hectic combat during which Bader was shot down and taken prisoner—he had carried out a total of 46 sorties over enemy territory and had claimed the destruction of six enemy aircraft, which brought him the award of the Distinguished Flying Cross. In the winter of 1941-2 No. 616 Squadron moved north for a rest, after which Johnson was given command of No. 610 Squadron at Ludham in Norfolk. From this airfield the squadron carried out numerous sweeps over Holland before moving to West Malling in August 1942, where No. 610 formed a wing together with the New Zealand 485 Squadron and the Canadian 411 Squadron.

No. 610 arrived at West Malling in time to take part in the first major combined operation of the war: Operation Jubilee, the landing at Dieppe. Six thousand troops—five thousand of them Canadians—went ashore at dawn on 19 August, with the fighter squadrons of the RAF maintaining an air umbrella overhead.

The Luftwaffe threw everything it had into the battle; squadrons of Messerschmitts and the redoubtable new Focke-Wulf 190s challenged the Spitfires over the burning beach-head and the Channel itself. The pilots of 610 made contact with the enemy fighters during their first sortie, and Johnnie sent down a 190 with a burst at maximum range. In the hectic fight that followed, during which his wingman was shot down, he found himself alone over Dieppe and engaging a lone Fw 190. The German pilot was no novice, and Johnson soon found himself fighting for his life; he tried every manoeuvre in the book, but was unable to shake off the enemy fighter. In the end he slammed open the throttle and dived over a British destroyer that was lying offshore, hoping that its flak would deter his pursuer. He sped across the warship and broke hard to port, looking back over his shoulder; there was no sign of the Focke-Wulf. He never knew if the German had been shot down or whether he had simply given up the chase.

Johnnie flew four sorties that day, during which the RAF lost two fighters for every German. It was a grim indication of the bitter air battles to come, for it was now apparent that in the Focke-Wulf 190 the enemy had a fighter that was superior on almost every count to the Mk. 5 Spitfires with which the majority of RAF Fighter Command's first-line squadrons were at that time equipped. Throughout the spring months of 1943 the Spitfire units received a severe mauling at the hands of their adversaries, and it was not until the advent of the more powerful Spitfire Mk. 9 that the balance was restored.

In March 1943 Johnson, newly promoted to Wing Commander, was posted to Kenley to lead a Canadian fighter wing, equipped with Spitfire 9s. His first victory with the wing was scored on 3 April, when the formation he was leading encountered Focke-Wulf 190s while escorting Typhoon fighter-bombers on a strike across the Channel. The Spitfires dived on the enemy formation and Johnson picked on the Focke-Wulf on the extreme left. He missed with his first burst, but the second hit the enemy fighter behind the cockpit and on the wing root. The Focke-Wulf dropped away, burning.

During his tour with the aggressive Canadian wing, Johnson's victories mounted rapidly. On 5 April he damaged three more 190s, shot down another on 11 May, and shared one with other Spitfire pilots on 13 May. During the next two weeks he destroyed another 190 and claimed a share in a Messerschmitt 109. More Focke-Wulfs fell to his guns on 15, 17, 24 and 27 June, followed by a trio of Messerschmitts on 15, 19 and 25 July. On the last day of the month he shared a 109 and on 12 August he shared another, together with one damaged. On 17 August he and three other pilots combined to shoot down a Messerschmitt 110—the first twin-engined aircraft Johnson had fired at. Another Messerschmitt 109 went down on 23 August, followed by Focke-Wulf 190s on 26 August and 4 September. Johnnie's personal score now stood at twenty-five enemy aircraft destroyed. His decorations included the DSO, DFC and Bar, and the American DFC—awarded for his week in leading the Canadian wing on escort duties with the bombers of the US Eighth Air Force. During his six-month tour with the Canadians he had led the wing on 130 sorties, and his pilots had destroyed over one hundred enemy machines.

In the autumn of 1943 the authorities, noting that the strain of continual combat was beginning to make its mark on Johnson, took him off operations for several months and assigned him to a staff job at the HQ of 11 Group Fighter Command. He remained there until March 1944, when he was posted to RAF Digby to take command of another wing composed entirely of Canadians: No. 144, which was then in the process of formation. In addition to its primary role of air fighting No. 144 was classified as a fighter-bomber wing; the Allied invasion of Europe was in the offing, and once air superiority had been established over the beach-heads the Spitfires would be employed on strafing and dive-bombing operations.

After two weeks of hard training at Digby the wing— consisting of Nos 441, 442 and 443 Squadrons—moved to an airfield near Bournemouth, from where the pilots carried out their first offensive sweep over occupied France. It was an unqualified success; the Canadians found a dozen enemy aircraft on the airfield at Dreux, near Paris, and left them in flames. Shortly afterwards the wing moved to Tangmere, and it was while operating from this location that Johnnie reopened his score, destroying two Fw 190s on 25 April.

D-Day, on 6 June 1944, found Johnson leading his wing on patrol over the Normandy beaches. For the Allied fighter pilots, thirsting for action, this first day of the invasion proved to be a bitter anti-climax. No. 144 wing made four sorties over the Channel between dawn and dusk, without once sighting the enemy. They were out of luck on subsequent days, too; the Luftwaffe was sighted on odd occasions, but the Spitfires were assigned to rigid patrol lines over the beaches and were unable to venture inland to make contact with the elusive enemy.

On 8 June, Johnson received orders from HQ 11 Group to take his wing to Normandy, where a temporary airstrip had been constructed at St Croix. Within forty-eight hours the Canadians were established in France and ready for operations—the first RAF fighter pilots to operate from French soil since 1940. The wing now formed part of No. 83 Group, Second Tactical Air Force, whose signals personnel had already built up the first links of what promised to be a highly effective fighter control system in Normandy during the brief period since the Allied landings. Under its guidance, the Spitfires of 144 wing would be able to range deep into France, their radius of action far outstripping that of the fighter squadrons still based in England. The Canadians kept one of their three squadrons always in readiness in case enemy air activity was detected by 83 Group's advanced radar.

As June wore on, the Luftwaffe once more began to appear in strength. On 16 and 22 June Johnnie added two more Focke-Wulfs to his score, followed by two Messerschmitt 109s on the 28th, another on the 30th and a fourth on 3 July. The enemy now began to appear in large formations of up to fifty aircraft, and on several occasions the pilots of 144 Wing encountered forty or fifty Messerschmitts led by a solitary 'long-nose' Focke-Wulf 190D-9. From intelligence sources, it was established that this machine—the latest variant of the German fighter—was flown by a renowned enemy pilot named Matoni.

The Spitfire pilots of 144 Wing were eager to come to grips with Matoni, and whenever they took off they were in the habit of asking control if there was any news of him in the vicinity. It was not long before the newspapers got hold of the story, and journalistic licence turned the whole affair into a personal challenge between Johnnie Johnson and his German opposite number. Johnson laughed off the ludicrous idea—but there was to be an amusing sequel. Not long after the end of the war, when Johnson was stationed in Germany, he received a letter from Matoni, who was then living in the Ruhr. Apparently the story had found its way into the German newspapers, too. Matoni was apologetic, explaining that he had been shot down and had therefore been unable to accept Johnson's 'challenge'. However, it was not too late

for honour to be satisfied, if the Englishman felt so in-
clined. . . .

Johnnie wrote back, explaining the real position and invit-
ing Matoni to come and have dinner one night in the
officers' mess at Lübeck, but the German never turned up.

Meanwhile, the bitter fighting in France continued. After
the breakout from Normandy No. 144 Wing was disbanded
and its units shared out among the RAF's other two Canadian
Spitfire Wings. Johnson went to command one of these, No.
127, and immediately plunged into the fierce battle for
Falaise, where the rapid Allied advance had trapped the
German Seventh Army. The latter, desperately retreating
through a narrow gap in the Allied encirclement, was now
being systematically cut to pieces by constant air attack. In
an endeavour to protect the harassed German troops the
Luftwaffe, operating from bases in the Paris area, put up a
fighter screen over the River Seine, and it was not long before the Spitfires were in contact with it. It was during one
of the subsequent air battles that Johnson had the closest
shave of his flying career, as he later described:

We came on at least a hundred Jerries, stepped up from ground
level to 8,000 feet in several layers. I got two and then remembered
that I had no faithful No. 2 guarding my tail, as he had turned back
with engine trouble shortly after we took off. I was about to nip away
when one of my flight commanders called up and asked me if I was
all right. I gave him my rough position and he said that he was in the
same area at 5,000 feet with his flight of six aircraft, and that he would
waggle his wings so that I could pick him out. I saw six aircraft 3,000
feet above me, and one was waggling its wings. I assumed they
must be the boys and I climbed rapidly towards them. I was only some
300 feet off when, to my horror, I saw dirty black crosses—they were
109s!

I peeled away and dived to the ground, but they had spotted me.
The chase was on. As they came streaking down, I turned violently to
port and kept my Spitfire turning as tightly as I possibly could. For a
few minutes we all spun round in a merry circle of perhaps half a
mile in diameter. The Hun leader then put two 109s on either flank

and left two more still turning with me, so that although the pair behind could not get a bead on me the other two chaps on the flank could come in with the occasional burst.

I could not continue turning indefinitely, so, opening the throttle wide, I tried another manoeuvre—a steep climb into the sun. The two German pilots stuck grimly behind me and as I reached 3,000 feet I could see their exploding cannon shells near my plane. So round to port again for a couple of quick turns and then up into the sun once more. But they were still on my heels. Then I felt my Spit shudder as she took a cannon shell in the starboard wing root.

I realised that my only hope was to try to climb to 12,000 feet where my supercharger would automatically cut in and give me the additional power I so badly needed if I was ever going to get the edge on the Huns. And so the battle went on: a few turns and then a flat-out climb straight into the sun, some more turns and another bout of climbing. . . . Immediately I sensed that they were about to open fire, I had to level out and start turning. Occasionally I got in a burst at them, but it was more of a gesture than a determined attack.

After what seemed an age, but was in fact I suppose only four or five minutes from when the Huns first spotted me, the supercharger automatically cut in. I nearly shouted for joy. I'd made it. The 109s were still with me, but now I knew that I had them licked. I had the extra power and a greater rate of climb. The Spit streaked away. I looked back and saw with relief and delight that I was easily outstripping them, but I didn't waste any time getting back to base.

It was the only time, in over four years of combat flying, that Johnson's aircraft was hit by enemy fire.

A few weeks later, Johnnie scored his thirty-eighth and last victory. He was patrolling the Rhine with twelve Spitfires between Arnhem and Nijmegen on 27 September 1944 when nine Messerschmitts were sighted, flying in the opposite direction. The Spitfires had the advantage of height, speed and surprise; it was the perfect bounce, and Johnson quickly sent a 109 down with one short burst. Within minutes the Spitfires were turning for home, leaving the burning wrecks of half a dozen enemy fighters scattered over the drab countryside.

During the winter of 1944-5 the wing, based at Evere in Belgium, was heavily engaged in ground-attack work as the

Allies fought hard to stem the last-ditch German offensive in the Ardennes. By the end of January 1945 the enemy had been shattered and the Allies were gearing up for Operation Varsity, the crossing of the Rhine. As this great operation unfolded in March Johnnie Johnson was promoted to Group Captain and posted to Eindhoven to take command of 125 Wing, equipped with three squadrons of new Spitfire Mk. 14s. Johnson led 125 Wing until the end of the war in Europe, and during those last desperate weeks his pilots—probing as far afield as Berlin—destroyed 140 enemy aircraft of all types.

After hostilities ended Johnson reverted to the rank of Wing Commander and took up an appointment as oc Tactics Branch at the Central Fighter Establishment. Following a year's course at the Canadian Staff College in Toronto from 1947-8 he went to the United States as an exchange officer with Tactical Air Command, and during this period he spent three months in Korea flying F-80 Shooting Star jets. In 1952 he was once more promoted Group Captain and given command of RAF Wildenrath, in Germany, a top fighter station within the Second Tactical Air Force. From 1954-7 he was Deputy Director of Operations at the Air Ministry, and during the next three years he commanded RAF Cottesmore in Rutland, home of the RAF's first Victor V-Bomber Wing. Promoted to Air Commodore in 1960, his next appointment was Senior Air Staff Officer at HQ No. 3 Group Bomber Command, and from 1963-5, until his retirement, he was Air Officer Commanding Air Forces Middle East, with the rank of Air Vice Marshal.

It was a career of which to be justly proud; and yet, concerning his wartime score, Johnnie Johnson modestly admits that he always fought with a squadron or a wing at his back —unlike the aces of the Battle of Britain such as 'Sailor' Malan and Douglas Bader, who scored their victories against overwhelming odds. He admits, too, that men such as these had already done most of the groundwork—

formulating the tactics that were to govern RAF fighter operations during the later years of the war—by the time he entered combat.

So it may be; but a man who can destroy thirty-eight of his enemies in four years of war, and sustain damage to his own machine only once in the process, possesses a skill that is rare even among the higher ranks of the fighter aces.

4 Pattle—the Forgotten Hero

The pilot lay in the low hollow between two dunes, his body pressed full length against the burning sand. The furnace of the desert sun beat down on him, torturing him with thirst. Yet he dare not move—for only a few yards away, their voices loud in the silence, was an Italian patrol. The pilot had seen their vehicle approaching in a cloud of dust and had immediately taken cover; the Italians had stopped on the other side of the dune and had not spotted him.

After what seemed an age, they climbed back into their truck and drove away. The pilot lay still until he could no longer hear the sound of the engine, then rose to his feet and resumed his long, exhausting trudge towards the British lines.

For Flight Lieutenant Marmaduke St John Pattle, 4 August 1940 had been a day of mixed fortunes. It had begun early that morning, when he and three other pilots had taken off in their Gloster Gladiator biplane fighters from No. 80 Squadron's base at Sidi Barrani to escort a slow-flying Lysander observation aircraft. The Lysander completed its mission successfully and lumbered away safely over friendly territory, while the Gladiators climbed over the front line to look for some action.

The enemy found them first. The first indication Pattle had of danger was when machine-gun bullets ripped through his aircraft's wings and an Italian Fiat CR.42 fighter shot past, diving out of the sun. Pattle and the other Gladiator pilots broke into a hard climbing turn, finding themselves confronted by a whole swarm of enemy machines—at least 17 CR.42s and 10 Breda 65 light bombers. One of the latter drifted into Pattle's sights, and he saw his bullets stitch a line of holes along the enemy's green-camouflaged fuselage. Thick smoke poured from its engine and the Breda nosed over into a dive. At the last moment the Italian pilot regained a measure of control and the bomber hit the ground heavily on its belly in a cloud of sand.

An instant later, Pattle loosed off a short burst at a Fiat that came into his sights. It was excellent deflection shooting, the enemy fighter began to trail smoke immediately and went down in a vertical dive. Then Pattle's own aircraft shuddered as bullets tore into it; the controls went sloppy and lifeless in his hands and the Gladiator spun down, out of control. There was no alternative but to bale out. He drifted down under the silken canopy and made a safe landing as the battle raged overhead. Discarding his parachute, he took his bearings from the sun and began to walk in the direction of the British lines.

No one had seen him bale out, and when his aircraft failed to return to Sidi Barrani he was listed as missing, believed killed. But Pattle was still very much alive, and although he twice narrowly escaped capture by Italian patrols during his walk across the sands he was picked up by a British patrol some twenty-four hours after he was shot down, arriving back at Sidi Barrani the next day. His latest taste of action had won him two more victories—and had made him a wiser man. From now on, he would make certain that no enemy caught him unawares.

Pattle—known simply as 'Pat' to his friends—was born in Butterworth, Cape Province, South Africa in 1913. He came from a strong military background, and as soon as he had completed his education at Graemian College, Grahamstown, he joined the South African Air Force as a cadet. To his great disappointment, however, he was not accepted for aircrew training, so he returned to civilian life and worked for some time with a mining company.

In 1936, with the urge to fly strong in him, he made his way to England and applied to join the Royal Air Force. He was quickly accepted, and soon showed that he had the makings of a born pilot. His aerobatics and marksmanship were excellent, and in 1937 he graduated from flying training school in the top three of his course. As a newly-commissioned Pilot Officer he was posted to No. 80 Squadron, which was equipped with Gloster Gladiator fighters, and during the following months he took part in many close formation aerobatic displays, an activity for which No. 80 was famous during the years immediately before the Second World War.

In 1938, with the international situation deteriorating rapidly, No. 80 Squadron was posted to Egypt to strengthen the RAF's air defences in the vital Suez Canal Zone. It was still there on the outbreak of war in September 1939, by which time Pattle was a flight commander. Throughout the spring of 1940 the squadron kept up its dull routine of patrolling the canal, interspersed with tactical exercises and air firing. In Norway and France, other RAF fighter squadrons were battling in a vain attempt to wrest air superiority from the Luftwaffe, and the fighter pilots of the Middle East squadrons chafed at the lack of action.

Their turn, however, was soon to come. On 10 June 1940, with the Battle of France irrevocably lost, Italy declared war on the Allies. In North Africa, the Italians had some 200,000 troops massed in their coastal provinces; opposing them the Allied forces amounted to 50,000 men, who were responsible both for internal security and the defence of Egypt's western frontier. The Italians also enjoyed numerical air superiority, and they possessed modern fighter aircraft which—in theory at least—outclassed the RAF's elderly Gladiators.

Immediately on the Italian declaration of war, British and

Commonwealth ground forces moved up the coast road to take up positions along the Libyan frontier, air cover being provided by the Gladiators of 33 Squadron. During the next couple of weeks No. 33's pilots saw considerable action and destroyed several enemy aircraft for no loss to themselves, but on 29 June one of 33's flight commanders was wounded in action and Pattle was temporarily detached from 80 Squadron to take his place.

Pattle's first serious taste of action came on 24 July, when six Gladiators led by the South African encountered eighteen Italian fighters and bombers over Sollum. Pattle destroyed one and the other Gladiator pilots accounted for three more without loss to themselves. The next day Pattle and three other Gladiators intercepted seven enemy aircraft over Bardia and destroyed five of them, Pattle himself shooting down three.

On 1 August No. 33 Squadron moved back to Helwan and its place at Sidi Barrani was taken by No. 80, Pattle rejoining his old unit. The squadron's equipment left much to be desired, consisting of seventeen elderly Gladiator Mk. Is and a small number of Mk. IIs 'borrowed' from the Egyptian Air Force. The squadron spent its first week at the front escorting the reconnaissance Lysanders of No. 208 Squadron, and sustained its first combat losses; on 4 August, the day Pattle was shot down, one Gladiator pilot was killed and another had to take to his parachute.

Four days later, however, the squadron had its revenge. On 8 August, thirteen Gladiators—including Pattle—were carrying out an offensive patrol when twenty-seven Fiat CR.42 biplanes were sighted near El Gobi. The Gladiators had all the advantages, attacking out of the sun, and in the whirling dogfight that followed nine Italian aircraft were destroyed for certain—two of them by Pattle. Six more Fiats were claimed as probably destroyed. One Gladiator pilot was killed and a second baled out safely.

The losses being inflicted on Mussolini's vaunted Regia

Aeronautica were more than the Italians could comfortably sustain, and during the remainder of August enemy aircraft ventured over the front less frequently, and as the Italian ground forces under Marshal Graziani attempted to concentrate men and equipment for an attack towards the Suez Canal—an attack that was to be broken by General Wavell's army before it got seriously under way—they were subjected to continual harassment by Allied aircraft.

Now, however, a new threat materialized as Mussolini launched a sudden attack on Greece from Italian-occupied Albania. Since the Balkans came under the sphere of responsibility of Air Chief Marshal Longmore, the Air Officer Commanding-in-Chief Middle East, steps were immediately taken to send RAF squadrons in support of the Greek forces, who were poorly equipped and hard pressed. Although they could ill be spared from the desert campaign, Longmore decided to despatch three squadrons of Blenheims and two of Gladiators—Nos 80 and 112. The task of the Blenheims would be to defend Athens, while the Gladiators flew in support of the Greek Army at the front.

No. 80 Squadron was the first to arrive in November, moving up to Paramythia in north-west Greece, close to the Albanian frontier, with sixteen Gladiator Mk. IIs. This airfield, however, was found to be too congested, with little provision for fuel and supplies, and early in December the squadron moved to a new location at Trikkala, from which base the Gladiator pilots were able to intercept enemy aircraft *en route* to attack Athens as well as carry out ground-attack missions and patrol the front line.

Already, during operations in November, Pattle had increased his score by destroying two Fiat CR.42s, sharing two more with other pilots and damaging two SM 79 bombers. On 2 December he shot down two Ro 37 observation biplanes, and on the 4th he destroyed three CR.42s, also claiming a fourth probably destroyed and a fifth damaged. On the 20th he claimed two more bombers—an SM 79 and an SM 81—and the next day he added another CR.42 to his list. Pattle's growing reputation as a superlative air fighter—a brilliant tactician who launched his attacks with split-second timing and who rarely missed—had an electrifying effect on the morale of the other pilots. By the end of December the squadron had destroyed no fewer than forty Italian aircraft for the loss in action of only six Gladiators, and the rumour that No. 80 would shortly re-equip with Hawker Hurricanes brought a promise of even greater achievements to come.

Nevertheless, it was with its ageing Gladiators that No. 80 Squadron entered the new year of 1941. During January air activity on both sides was severely curtailed by bad weather, but on the 28th three Gladiator pilots—one of them Pattle—shared in the destruction of a Cant Z.1007 bomber. Shortly afterwards, there was an impromptu party in the squadron's mess tent; the award of Pattle's Distinguished Flying Cross had just come through.

At the end of the month the squadron returned to Para-mythia, a move that coincided with an improvement in the weather and a consequent stepping-up of air action. There was a big squadron effort on 7 February, when the Gladia-tors encountered nearly forty CR.42s over the front line near Yannina; the British pilots shot down four of the enemy and claimed three more probably destroyed, although Pattle did not score on this occasion. Two days later, however, he en-joyed a further success when he claimed a CR.42; this was followed, on 10 February, by an air battle in which he dam-aged a Cant Z.1007 and also a BR.20 bomber.

It was Pattle's last action in the cockpit of a Gladiator. On 7 February the first Hurricanes had arrived in Greece, and these were immediately allotted to Pattle's 'B' Flight of No. 80 Squadron. The South African's first combat in a Hurri-cane took place on 20 February, when Pattle's flight was at-tacked by a squadron of Fiat G.50 fighters while providing escort for thirty Blenheims. The British pilots promptly showed how well they could handle their new aircraft by shooting down four of the enemy in as many minutes, Pattle himself making short work of the Italian leader.

By this time the Italian drive into Greece had become hopelessly bogged down in the face of the Greek Army's determined stand, and the Allies knew with grim certainty that it was only a question of time before the Germans took an active part in the campaign in order to save Mussolini's face. Before this happened the Greeks were anxious to win as much ground as possible, and in the last week of February 1941 they launched a major offensive that was designed to push the Italians out of Albania. The RAF fighter squadrons supporting the Greek Army—Nos 33, 80 and 112—flew almost non-stop during this phase, and it was while providing top cover for the Greek drive on Tepelini on 27 February that the British pilots scored their biggest success of the campaign. In just ninety minutes of air combat, two of the RAF squadrons—Nos 33 and 80—destroyed twenty-seven enemy aircraft over the front line, every one of them a confirmed victory.

Pattle, who had knocked down a CR.42 the day before, was in the thick of the fighting right from the start. After shooting down two more CR.42s he was forced to land to refuel and rearm, but when he took off again he saw that the battle was still raging. Climbing hard, he sighted three CR.42s over Valona and manoeuvred for an attack out of the sun. The Italians had not seen him, and Pattle dived on their tails, opening fire at close range and observing his bullets striking all three. The leading CR.42 went into a steep dive and Pattle followed it, giving it a second burst. It finally burned and plunged into the sea. Climbing and turning to face the other two enemy fighters, he was just in time to see them both spinning down trailing smoke, with their pilots' parachutes drifting overhead. The whole action had taken less than three minutes.

The next day Pattle shot down a pair of Fiat BR.20s, and

on 4 March he was involved in another big fight while leading his Hurricane flight on an offensive patrol over Himara. The pilots sighted and attacked a mixed formation of Fiat CR.42s and G.50s; on his first firing pass Pattle hit one of the latter in the fuel tank and the enemy fighter exploded, blazing fragments cascading earthwards from a spreading cloud of black smoke. Breaking hard to port Pattle found himself nicely placed behind a pair of CR.42s, one of which went into a steep climbing turn. A short burst from the Hurricane's guns and the Fiat went down, smoking; the pilot baled out. The other CR.42, throttle wide open, dived to ground level and tried to get away by hedge-hopping. For two minutes the Italian and his relentless pursuer leapfrogged over trees and hills, until a burst from Pattle found its target and the enemy biplane dived into the ground with a big explosion. The Hurricane was caught in the blast wave and slightly damaged by flying debris, but Pattle reached base safely.

Soon afterwards, Pattle was awarded a Bar to his DFC. He celebrated this on 24 March by shooting down a G.50, probably destroying another, and setting three more on fire during an attack on an enemy airfield. A few days later, he was posted to command No. 33 Squadron. Pattle had been with his new unit less than a week when, literally overnight, the battle situation took a dramatic turn for the worse. On 6 April 1941 German forces simultaneously invaded both Yugoslavia and Greece, and from dawn onwards the RAF fighters began to encounter the formidable Messerschmitt 109 in increasing numbers. From now on it would be no picnic, for against the 1,200 combat aircraft of the German Luftflotte 4 the Allies could muster only about 200 machines, and of these only about 50 were modern Hurricanes.

Despite their numerical inferiority the RAF pilots fought valiantly, and Pattle's score continued to grow. On the first day of the German invasion he destroyed two Messerschmitt 109s and other pilots of 33 Squadron accounted for three more for no loss to themselves. The next day Pattle shot down a CR.42, and on the 8th he knocked out a pair of 109s during a 'strafe' on an enemy airfield. On the 9th he shot down his first German bomber, a Junkers 88; on the 10th a Messerschmitt 109 and 110; on the 11th a Heinkel 111 and a Junkers 88; and on the 12th a Dornier 17 and an SM 79. Nevertheless, the enemy advance continued relentlessly and by the middle of April the Greeks and the Commonwealth forces supporting them were fighting a desperate withdrawal action, all the while under heavy air attack by the Luftwaffe. The RAF fighter squadrons did what they could, but the number of combat aircraft at their disposal dwindled steadily as the Luftwaffe launched determined raids on their airfields.

Finally, under overwhelming enemy pressure, it was decided to withdraw all the Hurricane squadrons to the Athens area in readiness to provide air cover for an evacuation of Allied forces, a possibility that was growing larger with every passing day. By this time there were only fifteen serviceable Hurricanes left in the whole of Greece, and these were assembled at Eleusis under Pattle's command.

Pattle himself was now suffering from extreme exhaustion, aggravated by a bout of influenza. Nevertheless he continued to fly and fight, and on 19 April he claimed two 109s and a Junkers 88 and shared a Henschel 126 observation aircraft with two other pilots. The next day, still feeling ill, he took off at the head of the surviving Hurricanes to intercept a formation of Junkers 88 dive bombers which was heading for Athens, escorted by a swarm of Messerschmitt 109s and 110s—over a hundred aircraft in all. Pattle led his Hurricanes right into the midst of the enemy, setting a 110 on fire with his first burst. A second 110 also went down in flames a few moments later, and as he climbed away Pattle found himself pursued by a pair of 109s. Throwing his Hurricane into a very tight turn he managed to get one of the enemy fighters in his sights and loosed off a short burst; the 109 fell apart as its fuel tanks exploded. Looking round, Pattle saw a lone Hurricane being harassed by two more 109s and turned to help. As he did so, he apparently made a serious omission —one that had almost cost him his life months earlier, when he had been shot down over the desert. He neglected to secure his tail. With eyes only for the aircraft ahead of him, he probably never even saw the Messerschmitt 110 that crept up behind him; at any rate, he took no evasive action. His Hurricane, riddled with cannon-shells, tumbled like a falling leaf into the waters of Eleusis Bay. The pilot did not bale out.

To this day, there remains some doubt as to Pattle's exact score of enemy aircraft destroyed. Some official sources put it at twenty-eight, others at thirty-four. Men who flew alongside him swear that it was over forty. No one will ever know for certain.

What is certain is that the exploits of 'Pat' Pattle, and the gallant pilots who fought against such overwhelming odds with such staggering success, will remain one of the finest chapters in the history of air warfare.

5 Richard Stevens— the Lonely Warrior

On the night of 15 January 1941, thousands of people in the London area must have looked up to see a long, white vapour trail spearing through the moonlit sky, threading its way through a maze of twinkling shell-bursts.

At the head of that slender white thread, lost in the darkness, was a Hawker Hurricane fighter. It was bitterly cold in the Hurricane's cockpit, and Flight Lieutenant Richard Stevens shivered in spite of his heavy fur-lined flying kit. Half an hour earlier, at 12.56 a.m., he had taken off from No. 151 Squadron's base at Manston as reports began to come in of enemy raiders heading for London. Now, at 15,000 feet, he could see the flashes of anti-aircraft shells ahead of him. Somewhere in that tortured area of sky was an enemy bomber.

Suddenly he saw it—the long, dark shape of a Dornier 17, flitting across the stars in a steep turn. Fierce exultation welled up inside Stevens; this was the moment he had been waiting for, ever since that terrible night several weeks earlier, when he had learned that his wife and children were lying dead beneath the rubble of their home following a night raid on Manchester. He screamed 'Tally-ho!' like a maniac over the radio, almost shattering the eardrums of the Manston controller, and went after the Dornier with throttle wide open.

The enemy bomber went into a fast climb up to 30,000 feet and levelled out. Stevens closed right in to less than fifty yards, waiting until the black bulk filled his sights before pressing the firing-button. Debris bounced off Stevens' aircraft and oil sprayed back on to the windscreen as the Dornier lurched and stalled. Stevens shoved the stick hard over, avoiding a collision by a hair's breadth. Looking round, he saw the Dornier hurtling earthwards and flung his Hurricane in pursuit. At three thousand feet the bomber pulled up sharply into a climbing turn. Stevens followed, blacking out momentarily under the high 'g', his fighter creaking and groaning as though on the point of falling apart.

When the black veil passed from his eyes Stevens saw that the Dornier was still climbing. He closed in quickly and loosed off a short burst, seeing the strikes dance and flicker on the Dornier's dark fuselage. Another burst, and lurid flames streamed back over the bomber's wings, lighting up the white-edged black crosses. Like a comet, the Dornier plummeted down and ripped into a wood, exploding among the trees in an enormous gush of flame. Stevens circled the spot, watching the bomber's funeral pyre turning the snow blood-red. Then he climbed away and set course for home. The Dornier was 151 Squadron's first night victory.

There was no sleep for Stevens that night. He sat in the crew-room at Manston, drinking scalding tea and hoping against hope that the Germans would come again. He was not disappointed. At 2 a.m., the harsh clamour of the telephone jerked him out of a doze. A few seconds later he was running for his Hurricane; more enemy raiders were heading for London. Within half an hour Stevens was at 17,000 feet, looking down at the tiny pinpricks of light that were actually huge fires raging in the heart of the capital. He circled endlessly, watching for the tell-tale anti aircraft bursts that would lead him to an enemy bomber. It seemed hopeless; the night sky was empty. Reluctantly, Stevens turned back towards Manston.

At that moment he sighted a target. It was a fat Heinkel 111, cruising along sedately at the same altitude. Stevens turned in behind it, coming up on the bomber's tail. Tracer flashed through the darkness as the Heinkel's rear-gunner opened up. Then Stevens' thumb jabbed down on the firing-button and the Hurricane's eight machine-guns roared, raking the Heinkel from wingtip to wingtip. Slowly, the bomber began to lose height. Dark bundles fell from it and two parachutes blossomed open, shining in the moonlight. Pouring smoke, the Heinkel spiralled down and crashed in the Thames Estuary. Stevens flew back to Manston, well satisfied with his night's work. He had become only the third RAF pilot to destroy two enemy aircraft in a single night, and the exploit was to earn him the DFC.

By any standard, Stevens was a veteran pilot. He was thirty years old—the maximum age for aircrew entry—when he joined the RAF at the outbreak of the Second World War, and his career as a fighter pilot began at an age when many pilots were finished with operational flying. His first squadron was No. 151, which he joined in October 1940 at the tail-end of the Battle of Britain, just as the Germans were beginning to switch their main attacks from daytime to night. It was in one of these early night raids that Stevens' family died, turning him into a dedicated killer.

No. 151, with its Hurricanes, was a day-fighter unit; its task ended when darkness fell. Night after night, as the enemy bombers droned towards London, Stevens would sit alone out on the airfield and watch the red glare of fires and the flicker of searchlights on the horizon, brooding and cursing the fact that the Hurricanes were not equipped for night-fighting. At last, one day in December, Stevens could stand the frustration no longer. He asked his commanding officer for permission to fly a lone night sortie over London, and it was granted.

Stevens had one valuable asset: experience. Before the war he had been a civilian pilot, flying the cross-Channel route with planeloads of mail and newspapers. He had amassed some four hundred hours' flying time at night and in all weather conditions, and his accumulated skill was soon to be put to good use.

His early night patrols were disappointing. For several nights running, although the Manston controller assured him that the sky was stiff with enemy bombers, Stevens saw nothing. Then came the memorable night of 15 January 1941, when he knocked two raiders out of the night sky.

At the time, night fighting was very much a hit or miss affair. Even the new airborne radar that was coming into service had more than its share of teething troubles, and first results were far from encouraging. But Stevens' first brace of kills seemed a good omen; after that, the raf's night fighter squadrons began to enjoy more success. Men like John Cunningham, flying fast twin-engined Beaufighters equipped with radar, began to carve out a reputation for themselves as bomber destroyers.

Stevens, however, stuck doggedly to his old Hurricane, stalking his victims alone through the night sky, aided only by the bursting anti-aircraft shells and by his own exceptional eyesight. He felt no special hatred, despite his personal loss, for the crews of the German bombers he shot out of the sky; they were just airmen like himself, following orders and doing a difficult job. But he loathed Hitler and the Nazis. Sometimes, as he poured bullets into a bomber's shattered cockpit, he would feel a sudden surge of pity for the young men he was killing. Then he would think what it would mean if the Nazis overran Britain—and he would feel savage elation as he watched the burning bomber plunge to destruction. His technique was to stalk an enemy bomber for minutes on end, finally closing in and firing at point-blank range to make sure of his kill. On one occasion, while pumping bullets into a Heinkel at a few yards' range, the bomber suddenly exploded in a violent gush of flame. The shock-wave flung the Hurricane over on its back and it shot through a cloud of blazing wreckage. Miraculously, the fighter was undamaged, but it was covered in oil and there was blood on the wings.

Shortly after the award of his first DFC, Stevens developed ear trouble and was grounded for a while. He returned to action with a vengeance on 8 April 1941, shooting down two Heinkel 111s in one night. Two nights later he got another Heinkel and a Junkers 88, and a few days later received a Bar to his DFC. He destroyed yet another Heinkel on the 19th, and on 7 May he accounted for two more. Three nights later his claim was one Heinkel destroyed and one probably destroyed. He shot down a further Heinkel on 13 June, damaged one on the 22nd and on 3 July sent a Junkers 88 down in flames. There seemed to be no end to his success; at this time he was the RAF's top-scoring night fighter, enjoying a considerable lead over pilots who flew the radar-equipped Beaufighters.

His victories were made possible not only by his experience, but also by a complete disregard for his own safety. He was like a man possessed, flying through violent anti-aircraft fire to get at his victims and opening fire from such close range that his Hurricane usually bore the scars of flying wreckage. He hated nights when he was earthbound; when the weather was too bad for even Stevens to fly he would wander round the officers' mess for a while, looking gloomy and not speaking to anyone. Finally, he would tuck himself away in a corner and lose himself in *The Seven Pillars of Wisdom*. For Stevens, Lawrence of Arabia—another lone wolf—was the greatest hero of all time.

He experienced a good deal of frustration during the summer months of 1941. In June the Germans invaded Russia, and by the end of July they had withdrawn many of their bomber units from the western front. Raids at night over Britain became fewer, and Stevens cursed and fidgeted at the lack of activity. For weeks, he never saw an enemy bomber.

Then, one evening in October, he spotted a Junkers 88

slipping inland over the coast of East Anglia and hurtled in to the attack. The 88 jettisoned its bombs and turned out to sea, diving low over the water in a desperate attempt to get away. It was hopeless; a short burst from Stevens' guns and the bomber sliced into the sea in a flurry of foam, leaving only a patch of oil and a few pieces of bobbing wreckage to mark its grave. It was Stevens' fourteenth victory.

Soon afterwards he was posted to No. 253 Squadron—another Hurricane unit—as a flight commander. After a few days with his new unit, an idea began to form in his mind. If he was unable to find enough enemy bombers in the night sky over Britain, why not slip over to France or Belgium under cover of darkness and shoot them down over their own airfields? The more he thought about the plan, the more he liked it. Finally, he obtained permission to give it a try.

Later in the war, intruder patrols—offensive sorties by RAF night-fighters over enemy airfields—were to become routine, but in December 1941 Stevens was virtually pioneering a new technique. On the night of 12 December, the day when the award of his DSO came through, the lone pilot took off in his Hurricane and set course out over the Channel. For an hour he flew in circles over the German bomber airfield of Gilze-Rijen, in Holland, waiting for an enemy aircraft to appear. But the bombers did not seem to be flying that night, and Stevens turned homewards in disappointment.

Three nights later, at twenty minutes to eight in the evening of 15 December, Stevens took off again and headed for the same destination. Slowly, the hours of the night dragged by. At Manston, his ground crew waited patiently for the sight of the familiar black-painted Hurricane slanting down out of the eastern darkness. They waited for hours, shivering in the cold, until long after all hope had vanished. This time, Richard Stevens would not be coming back.

The signal that his squadron commander sent to Group headquarters was simple and concise. 'One Hurricane IIC (long range), 253 Squadron, took off Manston 19.40 hours, 15.12.41, to go to Gilze. It has failed to return and is beyond maximum endurance.'

Years later, top-scoring RAF pilot Johnnie Johnson said of Stevens: '. . . To those who flew with him it seemed as if life itself was of little account to him, for the risks he took could only have one ending. . . . His end was inevitable, and after destroying at least fourteen enemy aircraft at night he failed to return from a patrol over enemy territory and was never seen again. We have the fondest memories of him.'

It was a fitting epitaph.

6 George Beurling— Malta Defender

In July 1944, a few weeks after D-Day, a score of leading Allied fighter pilots had a rendezvous at Catfoss, the RAF's Air Gunnery School in Yorkshire. They included such illustrious names as Group Captain A. G. 'Sailor' Malan, the Battle of Britain ace, and the American Richard Bong, fresh from his victories in the Pacific. Their task was to perfect new air fighting techniques in preparation for the great air battles to come over Germany.

One of those present was the famous French fighter pilot, Squadron Leader Pierre Clostermann, who later described his arrival at Catfoss in his book *Flames in the Sky*. When Clostermann walked into the anteroom of the officers' mess he found only one other occupant: an extraordinary figure in battledress, draped over an armchair and wearing no badges of rank or medal ribbons. Instead of a tie, he had a pair of silk stockings wound round his neck.

Clostermann sat down and fell asleep, to be awakened later by a raised voice. 'Who are you? Stand up! What the bloody hell are you doing here?'

Standing over the apparition in the armchair was a newcomer, also in battledress, his rank badges hidden by a flying jacket. The man in the armchair answered his question with two blunt syllables—at which the newcomer exploded and ordered him out of the room. The tone of authority had its effect; the man got up slowly, picked up a battered, oil-stained cap, and sauntered out.

Clostermann now recognized the man in the flying jacket; it was 'Sailor' Malan, who came over to welcome the Frenchman. 'Hullo, Clostermann, glad to see you again. Do you know who that was? Beurling, you know, the Malta type. I soon saw what his little game was. He was just waiting for some sprog P/O to tick him off so that he could tell him where he got off. He's been doing that every morning for a week in the waiting rooms at Air Ministry. But this time he picked the wrong bloke. I was shooting Jerries down while he was still in nappies. Anyway, it was a good lesson for him . . . he'll know now that he's got to behave himself here. But don't get him wrong, he really is a remarkable type.'

In describing Beurling, the word 'remarkable' was perhaps an understatement. Few fighter pilots are 'born', but George Beurling was one of them. He was also unruly and unorthodox, with a total contempt for rules that earned the displeasure of many a senior officer—and brought him to a pinnacle of success in air combat culminating in the destruction of twenty-seven enemy aircraft in the space of fourteen days in the embattled skies of Malta.

Beurling was born in Verdun, a suburb of Montreal, Canada, in 1922. When he was six years old his father built him a model aeroplane, and from that time on flying was young George's only fascination. By the time he was ten he was reading every book he could lay his hands on about the exploits of the fighter aces of the First World War, and spending most of his spare time watching aircraft at the local airport. His parents were disturbed by their son's growing obsession; his father wanted George to become a commercial artist, like himself, or as a second choice to study medicine.

The never-to-be-forgotten moment of his first flight came one day when, shortly before his eleventh birthday, he was caught in a violent rainstorm during one of his frequent excursions to the aerodome. A pilot, taking pity on the soaked boy, invited him to take shelter in a hangar, and—seeing George's obvious enthusiasm—offered to take him for a flight if the boy got his parents' consent. His father and mother thought he was joking, and said yes—and within hours George was airborne.

From then on, all his energies were devoted to saving his pocket money towards that day, as yet some years in the future, when he would be old enough to take flying lessons. He left no financial stone unturned; he sold newspapers on street corners in all weathers, he did all manner of odd jobs, he built model aircraft and sold them. When he was fifteen, against his parents' wishes, he left school and got a job—anything to earn enough money to become a pilot. He cut down his food and other living expenses to the absolute minimum, and at the end of each week he had just sufficient funds to buy himself an hour in the air. Sometimes he was able to add to his weekly flying time by doing odd jobs around the airfield.

When he was sixteen, with over 150 flying hours already under his belt, he passed all the examinations for a commercial pilot's rating—only to learn that he was still too young to be licensed. Undeterred, he determined to set out for China, then engaged in a bitter conflict with Japan; he had heard that pilots were desperately needed, and that the Chinese were not too particular about age limits. He crossed the border into the United States, heading for San Francisco with the idea of working his passage to China—but he was quickly arrested as an illegal immigrant and sent back home.

In September 1939 the Second World War broke out, and seventeen-year-old Beurling immediately applied to join the Royal Canadian Air Force as a pilot—only to discover that he lacked the necessary educational qualifications. He then volunteered for the Finnish Air Force, which was recruiting pilots urgently as tension grew with the Soviet Union, and was accepted—but he needed his father's consent, and this was not forthcoming. Bitterly disappointed, George continued to fly privately, and by the spring of 1940 he had logged 250 hours' solo flying. His sights were now set on joining the Royal Air Force as quickly as possible, and with this goal in mind he attended night school to bring himself up to the required academic standard.

In May 1940 he signed on as a deckhand aboard a Swedish freighter bound for Glasgow, where he reported to the nearest RAF recruiting centre as soon as he arrived. To his dismay, he was told that in order to be considered for the RAF he would need both his birth certificate and his parents' consent; he had neither. Undaunted, he sailed back to Canada and a week later he was making the eastbound trip across the Atlantic once more, armed with the necessary documents.

He was finally selected for flying training in the RAF on 7 September 1940, and a year later—with his pilot's wings proudly displayed on his left breast—he reported for operational duty with No. 403 Squadron as a Sergeant Pilot. For a time, he had found his niche; but then it was decided to make No. 403 an all-Canadian squadron, and since Beurling was an RAF pilot he was posted to another unit.

The new squadron placed a good deal more emphasis on the regulations than No. 403, and Beurling soon found himself very much an outsider. After three months, he volunteered for an overseas posting. So it was that, on 9 June 1942, Flight Sergeant George Frederick Beurling found himself strapped in the vibrating cockpit of a brand-new Spitfire Mk. V on the flight deck of the aircraft carrier HMS Eagle, preparing to launch off over the Mediterranean towards the island of Malta, which was then reeling under the combined hammer-blows of the Luftwaffe and the Regia Aeronautica, the Italian Air Force—their bombers operating from the packed air bases of Sicily, a mere seventy miles away from the besieged island.

The Canadian's arrival on Malta was dramatic. Seconds after he taxied his Spitfire clear of the runway at Luqa a big enemy raid developed and he was bundled unceremoniously into a slit trench while waves of Junkers 88s and Italian bombers pounded the airfield. Beurling watched the action unfolding all around him and exulted: this was war at last! After all his years of struggle, he would soon have a chance to come to real grips with the enemy.

The action was to come sooner than even he anticipated. At 15.30 that same afternoon he was strapped into the cockpit of his Spitfire on immediate readiness, with eleven other fighters of No. 249 Squadron ranged alongside him. The pilots, even though they wore only shorts and shirts, were dizzy with the heat as the sun beat down mercilessly; although it would be up to thirty degrees below freezing at 20,000 feet, to don heavier flying clothing would be to risk sunstroke on the island's baked surface.

It came as a relief when the Squadron was ordered to scramble to intercept an incoming raid over Gozo, Malta's neighbouring island. The Spitfires climbed in sections of four, their pilots searching the sky to the north. Suddenly they saw the enemy: twenty Ju 88s, escorted by forty Messerschmitts.

Beurling's section went for the fighter escort while the remaining Spitfires tackled the bombers. There was no time for manoeuvre; the opposing sides met head-on at 18,000 feet over the sea and within seconds a fierce dogfight spread out across the sky. George loosed off an ineffectual burst at a Messerschmitt that flashed across his nose; a moment later he got another enemy fighter in his sights, but at the last instant the Messerschmitt skidded out of the line of fire and dived away.

The next moment, Beurling himself came under fire and hurled his Spitfire into a violent turn. His adversary shot past him; it was an Italian Macchi 202 fighter, and now it hung squarely in Beurling's sights as the Canadian turned in behind it. The Macchi shuddered as the Spitfire's cannon shells struck home and then went down in a fast spin. There was no time to see whether the Macchi crashed; the sky was still full of twisting aircraft and, throttle wide open, Beurling went after a section of Junkers 88 bombers which was diving in the direction of Valetta harbour. Closing in to within fifty yards of the rearmost bomber he raked it with his cannon; the Junkers burst into flames and the crew baled out.

As he was preparing to select another target, Beurling heard a frantic call over the R/T from a fellow pilot who—short of fuel—was being prevented from landing on Safi airstrip by patrolling Messerschmitts. Beurling at once dived over the island towards Safi, squeezing off a short burst at a Messerschmitt on the way. It was a lucky shot; the German fighter spun down and crashed. Arriving over Safi, Beurling quickly assessed the situation. A lone Spitfire, desperately trying to land, was about to be given the *coup de grâce* by a Messerschmitt closing in on its tail. Beurling arced down and opened fire, roaring over the top of the landing Spitfire and attacking the Messerschmitt head-on. The enemy fighter flashed past him and vanished. A moment later, more Spitfires arrived and circled watchfully overhead as Beurling himself went in to land.

An hour later Beurling was airborne once again, together with every available fighter on the island, intercepting thirty Junkers 87 Stukas which were attacking the freighter *Welshman*, unloading a vital cargo of ammunition and fuel. The Spitfires and Hurricanes ran the gauntlet of their own flak to get at the Stukas as they dived over Valetta, and a massive free-for-all developed over the harbour as no fewer than 130 enemy fighters joined the fray. Beurling shot down a 109 and severely damaged a Junkers; pieces from the enemy bomber whirled back and smashed his propeller, but he pulled off a perfect bellylanding near the clifftops.

So ended George Beurling's first day on Malta. In less

than a couple of hours' air fighting he had opened his score-board with three enemy aircraft destroyed for certain and two 'probables'. It was a promising start.

During the remainder of June there was a comparative lull in the air fighting over Malta; the Germans and Italians had suffered considerable losses in the massive air attacks of April and May, which had all but beaten the island to its knees, and were now gathering their strength for a renewed offensive. In July, however, the fighting flared up once more, and on the 11th Beurling destroyed three Macchi 202s in the course of a single afternoon—an exploit that earned him the award of the Distinguished Flying Medal.

From then on, his score began to mount with remarkable speed. On the 18th he shot down a Reggiane 2001 fighter; on the 27th he destroyed two Macchis and two Messer-schmitts, damaging two more; and on the 29th he knocked down another Messerschmitt 109. He opened his August score on the 8th with yet another 109, and on the 13th he shared a Junkers 88 with two other pilots.

Beurling's success was attributable to three things in the main: his phenomenal eyesight, brilliant marksmanship and the fact that he preferred to do things his own way, rather than by the book. Since he was only an 'average' fighter pilot his eyesight was undoubtedly his most valuable asset, in this dangerous game where the ability to spot the enemy first was of life-or-death importance. Beurling's large, pale-blue eyes were his most striking feature, and he carried out constant exercises to improve his sight. One of these in-volved making a series of tiny pencil marks on the crew-room wall; he would sit in an armchair, facing the opposite way, then suddenly swivel round and try to locate the marks as quickly as possible. His eyesight, in fact, attained such a degree of perfection that he was usually able to state with absolute certainty how many cannon shells he had put into an enemy aircraft, and where they had struck home.

The rest of August and early September passed fairly

quietly, and Beurling saw no action. He became solitary and morose, and to add to his general depression he suffered badly from the 'Malta Dog', a form of dysentery that made being cooped up in the confines of a Spitfire's cockpit for any length of time an agonizing ordeal. During this period he was awarded a Bar to his DFM; he also acquired the nickname 'Screwball', which he detested. The story goes that he would throw a piece of meat on the ground and then stamp on the flies that settled on it, muttering 'Goddam Screwballs!' as he did so. This story may or may not be true; what is certain is that Beurling, although he may have been referred to as 'Screwball' by some sections of the popular Press, was always known to his friends as 'Buzz'—or simply George.

Before his arrival in Malta, while he was serving with 403 Squadron, Beurling had twice turned down the offer of a commission. He was, he maintained, not the officer type. On Malta, however, Beurling unconsciously became a leader; in combat, his ability to sight the enemy before anyone else drew other fighter pilots like a magnet. Wherever George Beurling was, action would not be far away. His superiors were quick to realize his potential, and one day he was informed that he was going to be commissioned, whether he liked it or not. George protested in vain, but it was a long time before he got round to sewing on his new officer's rank braid.

For most pilots, Malta was a nightmare. For George Beurling, it was the fulfilment of a dream. Here, in the embattled skies over the island, he found vindication for the days he had spent shivering in the winter snow of Montreal, selling newspapers, and later for the thinly-veiled sarcasm of more than one ground instructor at the RAF basic training school, Buxton-on-Sea, exasperated by the Canadian's lack of education compared with other students. George enjoyed every minute of Malta, and made no secret of the fact; where the average tour of a fighter pilot on the island in the middle of 1942 was three months, Beurling applied for an extension and got it.

Towards the end of September, with Malta's torpedo-bombers and submarines taking a growing toll of Rommel's vital supply lines to North Africa, the Germans made a last desperate attempt to knock out the island. There was fierce air fighting on the 25th, when Beurling destroyed a pair of Messerschmitt 109s. On 9 October he shot down three more, together with a Junkers 88, a score that was repeated three days later. On the 13th he got another 109, bringing his score to twenty-four. 15 October was another hectic day—and for George Beurling, the last day of combat on the island. He engaged a Junkers 88 and shot it down, but not before the enemy gunner had hit his Spitfire and wounded him in the heel. Despite this, he managed to shoot down two Messerschmitts before taking to his parachute. He landed in the sea and was picked up by an Air-Sea Rescue launch.

After a fortnight in hospital, his lengthy tour having finally expired, he boarded a Liberator bomber *en route* for England. There were thirty-nine people on the aircraft, mostly tour-expired pilots like himself. At Gibraltar, where the Liberator was due to refuel, some sixth sense warned George of impending disaster. As the bomber approached Gibraltar's runway through heavy turbulence, he took off his heavy flying jacket and moved to a seat near one of the emergency exits.

The approach was a poor one and the Liberator floated along half the runway before its wheels finally touched. The pilot opened the throttles to go round again and pulled the bomber into the air. The climb was too steep; at fifty feet the big aircraft stalled and plunged into the sea.

At the moment of the stall, Beurling jettisoned the escape hatch next to his seat, and as the bomber struck the water he dived out. Although his foot was still encased in plaster, he managed to swim one hundred and fifty yards to the shore. He was one of twenty-four survivors. After a further spell in hospital Beurling returned to Canada for a rest. He was feted as a national hero. Nevertheless, he was glad when, in the latter part of 1943, he returned to England for operational duty with No. 412 Squadron, which formed part of the wing commanded by 'Johnnie' Johnson. Soon after his return, he attended an investiture at Buckingham Palace and received from King George VI no fewer than four decorations at the same time: the DSO, DFC, DFM and the Bar to the DFM.

Beurling, ever the lone wolf, found it hard to reconcile himself with the tempo of air operations over western Europe after the hectic battles in Maltese skies. Although a flight commander with 412 Squadron, the fact that he was a relatively small cog in a wing of thirty-six Spitfires—which frequently carried out 'sweeps' over France without sighting a single enemy aircraft—made him feel insignificant. He failed to drum up much enthusiasm for the task assigned to him by Johnnie Johnson, that of wing gunnery officer. Johnson knew that Beurling had achieved most of his victories by tricky deflection shots, and wanted the Canadian to pass on his knowledge to less experienced pilots; but Beurling's style of air fighting was peculiar to his own temperament, and he found it difficult to hammer his techniques home to pilots already moulded in a more orthodox school.

Over France, Beurling encountered the redoubtable Focke-Wulf 190 fighter; he had already shot down one of these machines, while flying with 403 Squadron back in the early months of 1942, and before the end of 1943 he had added three more to his score, making a total of thirty-one and one-third confirmed victories—the 'one-third' being in connection with the Junkers 88 he had shared over Malta.

George's combat career, however, was almost over. More and more, he found himself involved in instructional duties —a trend that culminated, in the summer of 1944, with a posting to the gunnery school at Catfoss. Here, during preliminary air firing exercises, Beurling astonished everybody by achieving persistently low scores—and then, suddenly, he began to register a success rate of close on one hundred per cent. He explained that, during the earlier exercises, he had been trying to follow 'the book'. Since he was not having much success, he had reverted to his own unorthodox methods—and the improvement was dramatic.

The end of the war found Beurling with the rank of Squadron Leader. By this time he had officially transferred to the Royal Canadian Air Force, and demobilization quickly followed the end of hostilities. For two years after the end of the war George drifted from one job to another. He flew commercially, toured the country as a stunt pilot, and even sold life insurance—which he loathed. He was completely unable to adjust to civilian life, yearning all the while for a return to the heady thrill of combat and the comradeship of a front-line squadron.

Early in 1948, it seemed that his prayers had at last been answered. The infant state of Israel, on the point of declaring her independence and threatened on all sides by her Arab neighbours, was scouring the western world for combat aircraft and pilots. George heard that several ex-RCAF fighter boys had already volunteered, and lost no time in offering his own services. The Israelis were operating Spitfires; it would be good to squeeze into that narrow, vibrating cockpit once more.

On 18 May, a couple of days after Israel's declaration of Independence, George arrived at Rome's Urbe airport. On the 20th, he was detailed to fly a planeload of medical supplies over the last lap to Israel. The aircraft was a Noorduyn Norseman, a type with which Beurling was unfamiliar. A former Canadian Naval pilot named Cohen offered to do a few circuits with him to check him out. Eyewitnesses saw the aircraft take off, circle the field, and approach to land. The engine roared as it overshot the runway and began to climb away. A few moments later, it stalled and dived into the ground. Both occupants were killed instantly.

Flying had been George Beurling's life, and his death. He was twenty-six years old.

7 Robert S. Johnson— Thunderbolt Pilot

In the story of the air war over Europe, 6 March 1944 was a significant date. On that day, 660 B-17 and B-24 heavy bombers of the United States Eighth Air Force struck at Berlin for the first time in daylight. From now on, the German capital would feel the full weight of the Allied air offensive round the clock; the Lancasters and Halifaxes of RAF Bomber Command by night, the Fortresses and Liberators by day.

The American pilots had been waiting for this moment. A year earlier, when the Eighth had first begun its daylight attacks on German targets, the lack of long-range fighter escort had made raids on objectives requiring deep penetration out of the question; losses sustained during attacks on 'fringe' targets in German territory had been heavy enough as it was. Now it was different. In the P-51 Mustang the Americans had a fighter with sufficient range to escort the bombers all the way to Berlin and back, with sufficient reserves of fuel for combat over the target; the P-47 Thunderbolt could reach Berlin too, although its endurance was not so great as the Mustang's. Squadrons equipped with the third American fighter type, the Lockheed P-38 Lightning, could undertake effective escort as far as the German border.

One of the Thunderbolt units assigned to the Berlin mission of 6 March was the 56th Fighter Group, based at Halesworth in Suffolk. Comprising three fighter squadrons—the

61st, 62nd and 63rd—it was commanded by Colonel Hubert Zemke and numbered several of the top-scoring fighter pilots in the European Theatre. Leading them was Lieutenant Robert S. Johnson of the 61st Squadron, with over twenty victories to his credit.

Sixteen years earlier, almost to the day, eight-year-old Bob Johnson had stood with the crowd of spectators on Post Field, Oklahoma, and watched in fascination as the barnstorming pilots of 1928—most of them veterans of World War I—threw their biplanes round the sky with effortless mastery. There and then, Bob had made up his mind: he was going to be a pilot. Nothing else would satisfy him.

It was not an easy path he had chosen. As a youth in his home town of Lawton he worked in a cabinet-making shop for just four dollars a week, and exactly one-third of it went to pay for a fifteen-minute flying lesson every Sunday morning. Thirty-nine dollars and six and a half hours' flying time later he made his first solo flight, and thought he knew everything about flying. Sixteen years later, with over a thousand hours and a lot of combat experience behind him, he was to admit that the learning process was only just beginning.

In September 1941 Johnson entered college in Texas; he had been there less than two months when he gave it up and joined the US Army Air Corps as an aviation cadet. Flight training showed him to be an above-average pilot, but in other subjects he came close to failure. This was particularly true of air gunnery, which he never succeeded in mastering during his training, and his low score in this subject made him in theory more suited to the role of bomber pilot. For this reason, on completion of his basic training in 1942, he was posted to an advanced flying school operating twin-engined trainers.

Johnson, however, was prepared to work hard to overcome his deficiencies, and by the middle of 1942 his gunnery had improved to such an extent that he was able to apply successfully for a transfer to single-seat fighters. He was assigned to the 56th Fighter Group, which was then working up to full operational status under 'Hub' Zemke's dynamic leadership. The 56th arrived in England on 13 January 1943, but it was some weeks before it received its full complement of forty-eight Thunderbolts and it was not until the spring that operational flying began in earnest. Johnson's first taste of action came in April, when the Group was escorting a small B-17 raid. He was flying No. 4 to Zemke when the P-47s were bounced by eight Focke-Wulf 190s. Johnson opened fire at one of them and missed, but registered hits on a second 190 that flashed through his sights.

The chance to score his first victory did not present itself until June 1943. Flying over northern France with the 61st Squadron, Johnson sighted twelve Fw 190s cruising a few thousand feet below. At that time, American fighter tactics generally involved waiting to be attacked first by the enemy —a policy with which the young pilot heartily disagreed. Exasperated, he broke formation and dived on the Focke-Wulfs, who failed to spot him until it was too late. Whistling through their formation at high speed he tore a 190 apart with a short burst from his six .5-calibre machine-guns, then climbed hard to rejoin formation. The remaining Focke-Wulfs followed him, and in the ensuing battle Colonel Zemke shot down two of them. Nevertheless, when he returned to base Johnson received a severe reprimand for breaking formation, and was told in no uncertain terms that if he did it again he would be grounded.

A few days later, while sticking rigidly to his station, he was almost shot down when the Thunderbolts were bounced by a squadron of Messerschmitts. It came as a considerable relief when, not long after this incident, the commander of the Eighth Air Force's fighter units—Major-General Anderson—sought and obtained approval for the adoption of more aggressive tactics. From now on, Johnson came into his own—and so did several other 56th Group pilots. In the months to come, 'Zemke's Wolfpack' was to count in its ranks some of the leading American fighter aces of World War II; Zemke himself was to end the war with seventeen victories, while several among the pilots introduced to combat by Zemke exceeded that score by a considerable margin; Bob Johnson and fellow pilot Francis Gabreski would go on to lead the field in the European Theatre with 28 kills apiece—Gabreski subsequently shooting down six more in jet combat over Korea—while Major Walker M. Mahurin and Colonel David C. Schilling were to notch up twenty-four and a half and twenty-two and a half respectively.

Bob Johnson's early months in combat were not spectacular; nevertheless, he formulated sound fighting tactics which ultimately were to pay high dividends. Next to Zemke, he became the man sought out by newcomers to the Group, eager to gain from his experience, and his advice to them was relatively simple: 'Never let a Jerry get his sights on you. No matter whether he is at 100 yards or at 1,000 yards away, a 20-mm will carry easily that far and will knock down a plane at 1,000 yards. It is better to stay at 20,000 feet with a good speed with a Jerry at 25,000 feet than it is to pull up in his vicinity at a stalling speed. If he comes down on you, pull up into him and nine times out of ten, if you are nearly head-on with him he'll roll away to his right. Then you have him. Roll on to his tail and go get him.'

These tactics saved his life time and again. One day in the high summer of 1943 Johnson's squadron was escorting B-17s in a raid on Kiel when the contrails of enemy fighters were sighted to the south. Johnson immediately pulled the lever to jettison his long range fuel tank, but it was jammed There was no time to worry about it now; fifteen Focke-Wulfs were diving on the bombers and Johnson's section turned to engage them.

'We went at the nearest ones head-on, and they broke for the deck. They kept coming and I kept hitting them head-on, driving them down. I was making my third pass when Hamilton (one of the pilots in Johnson's section) yelled over the R/T, "Get these bastards off my tail!" I still had that belly tank. I kept yanking at the release, and it wouldn't drop.

'Down below at 16,000 feet three planes were going round and round—two Fws on Hamilton. One would make a pass at him from the front while the other got on his tail. I put my ship in a dive but I couldn't pull out in time. That belly tank was interfering with the trim. As I pulled up, Hamilton did a turn-over and gave the gun to one of the Huns. He went down on fire, and Hamilton then got on the other's tail.

'It was a clear day. We were over the coast, the line of breakers curving white against the shore. People were watching from below. It must have been a good show, but the damned fools might have got hit. Hamilton didn't need any help from me any more, and I sat over and above him and his Hun, watching the fun. Hamilton got his second plane—and then I looked around and saw a Hun on my tail.

'As he came in on my tail, shooting, I did a tight climbing turn. The Jerry had the position—and I had that belly tank. He kept inside me, trying for a deflection burst. I held the turn until his nose dropped a bit. Then I slipped down and hit him.

'Then he was on me again and we went through the same thing. On this turn my belly tank finally dropped. When his nose dipped I came over and hit him again. We went through this four times, and it took ten minutes, which is a long, long time for a dogfight. Then his cockpit jumped into the air and the plane flew under it. He was coming apart, and I gave him another burst just to make sure of it.'

On the ground, Johnson was a quiet man. Apart from flying, his great loves were photography and wood carving—the latter a heritage from his cabinet-making days. He spent many hours making carved souvenirs for the other pilots in

the Group, and in his off-duty hours he was often to be seen
in the countryside around Halesworth, photographing the
English villages and rural scenes. He spent a lot of time with
the local people, and as a result his Oklahoma drawl became
mingled with the soft accents of Suffolk; it was a habit of
speech that was never to leave him.

His score continued to mount steadily, and in the spring
of 1944—by which time he was commanding the 61st Squadron—he became the first American pilot to equal the score
of the World War I ace, Eddie Rickenbacker, with twenty-
five kills. He was now running neck-and-neck with Richard
I. Bong, who was flying P-38 Lightnings in the Pacific with
the Ninth Fighter Squadron of the 49th Fighter Group.
Bong had achieved twenty-one victories by November 1943,
in the air battles over Milne Bay and Rabaul; he returned to
action early in 1944, after a short spell of leave, and by the
last week in February he had matched Johnson with twenty-
five kills.

As March dawned, Johnson eagerly awaited the first
deep-penetration mission to Berlin, with its promise of
major action; action which he hoped would at last give him
the chance to reach the magical figure of twenty-six kills
and be the first to surpass Rickenbacker. A bitter disappointment, however, was in store for him. On 5 March, the
day before the big raid finally got under way, news came
through from the Pacific that Dick Bong had got two more
Japs, bringing his score to twenty-seven.

There was still time to capture the lead once more. As the
pilots of the 56th assembled in the briefing room at Halesworth on that morning of 6 March the sky overhead was
clear, and the forecast covering the route was favourable.
The Luftwaffe was certain to be up in strength, and the
fighter pilots were going to need all their skill to shepherd
the bombers to the target and back. If the Group failed to
make contact with the enemy the pilots were briefed to attack ground targets on the way out of Germany, but it was

unlikely that they would have much time to engage in this
kind of activity. For the Berlin mission the 56th Fighter
Group was to be split into two echelons, each of thirty-five
machines; its strength had grown considerably since its arrival in England over a year earlier. Hubert Zemke would
lead the first echelon, Johnson the second.

At exactly 10.32 Johnson roared down Halesworth's runway in his red-nosed Thunderbolt, the name 'All Hell' em-
blazoned on its side, and climbed away in a wide left-hand
curve towards the east. The other thirty-five Thunderbolts
of his echelon followed him, sliding into formation on the
climb. Over to starboard, like a shoal of fat-bellied fish,
cruised Zemke's thirty-five P-47s.

The formation climbed to 27,000 feet over the North Sea
and made landfall over the island of Walcheren, crossing
the Zuider Zee into Dutch territory. The bombers were visi-
ble up ahead now, compact boxes of B-17s dragging their
broad vapour trails. As the distance narrowed Johnson's formation split into three units, one slipping into position
directly above the bombers and the others guarding their
flanks. As they approached the German border the unit on
the right flank of the B-17 formation—eight P-47s of the
62nd Squadron, led by Lieutenant Mike Quirk—suddenly
peeled off and went into a fast dive. A few moments later, a
confused babble of shouts and curses burst over the R/T as
Quirk's boys tangled with a group of Messerschmitt 109s
they had spotted climbing towards the bombers.

The remainder flew on into Germany, holding a steady
course for Berlin. The two remaining units of Johnson's
fighter formation now spread out to north and south of the
B-17s, the pilots quartering the sky carefully; the enemy
fighters would be coming in fast, and it was important to get
to grips with them as far out from the bombers as possible.

Johnson picked out a cluster of dots, approaching from
the north. Radial engines, short wings: P-47s. Then someone
gave a warning shout; they were not P-47s, they were

Focke-Wulf 190s, and close behind them came a second formation of Messerschmitt 109s. The Thunderbolts fanned out and turned to meet the enemy, but there was little they could do at this stage. The two fighter formations flashed past one another at a closing speed of over 600 mph, the Germans streaking towards the bombers. Johnson brought his Thunderbolts round in a hard turn on to the enemy's tail, the American pilots running into the fire of the B-17s' guns as they flashed in pursuit of the Germans through a sky now filled with the debris of bombers, torn apart by salvoes of rockets and 20-mm cannon shells, and drifting parachutes.

The Thunderbolts followed the enemy down into clear sky, overhauling them at 18,000 feet. Johnson closed on a section of Fw 190s from the rear, opening fire on the right-hand aircraft of the four. Pieces of engine cowling broke away and fluttered back in the slipstream, followed by the long, transparent cockpit canopy. An instant later, the German pilot baled out. Johnson looked around; his wingman was still sticking rigidly to him. Once again, the sky was a confusion of aircraft, either whirling in dogfights or falling in flames. Johnson got in a burst at a 190 that tried to get on his wingman's tail; the German sheered off and vanished. Two more 190s came down in a shallow dive, firing, and the pair of Thunderbolts turned to meet them. The four fighters closed head-on, their wings lit by twinkling flashes from their guns, and at the last moment both Focke-Wulfs rolled sharply away to the right. The Thunderbolts followed them, gaining rapidly, and the two enemy fighters split up. Johnson and his wingman went after the leader, who throttled right back in the hope of making the Thunderbolts overshoot and went into a steep turn to the left. It was an old trick, and if the German's adversary had been a less experienced pilot it might have worked. But Johnson throttled back too, turning with the 190. Gradually, the Focke-Wulf's shape crept into his sights; he was out-turning the enemy fighter. Johnson fired in short bursts, hitting the 190, which wavered and levelled out, entering a shallow dive once more. The American pulled round hard and came in on the 190's tail. Another burst and the Focke-Wulf began to trail smoke, diving into the ground and exploding.

The combat had taken the Thunderbolts almost to ground level, and as they climbed away they seemed to be alone in the sky. Then Johnson spotted a lone B-17, a straggler being harried by half a dozen German fighters. The P-47s went in to the attack and the enemy broke away, diving earthwards. Two more Focke-Wulfs flashed past and Johnson loosed off a burst at extreme range without hitting anything. There could be no question of giving chase, or of escorting the labouring B-17, for the Thunderbolts' fuel reserves were already marginal. Climbing away, the Thunderbolts set course for the North Sea and home, joining up with other fighters on the way. Behind them, scattered over the route to Berlin, lay the wreckage of sixty-nine American bombers and eleven fighters; the Germans had lost nearly eighty Focke-Wulfs and Messerschmitts. The battle of Germany had been joined in earnest.

Once again, Johnson and Dick Bong were level; they were still level at the end of March, when Johnson scored his twenty-eighth victory. All his kills had happened in only eleven months of combat flying, a unique achievement among American fighter pilots in the European Theatre.

Then the authorities decided that it was time for both Bong and Johnson to have a rest; they were too valuable to get themselves killed at this stage. Both were sent home, and for the next few months they toured the United States promoting the sales of war bonds—Johnson flying a P-47, Bong a P-38 Lightning.

Bob Johnson, who had completed two extensions of his combat tour in Europe, never returned to action. Bong, after spending a short time at the RAF's air warfare school in England, was posted back to the Pacific on the headquarters staff of V Fighter Command—a job that was not supposed to involve combat flying. But Bong got into action whenever he could, and went on to shoot down twelve more Japanese aircraft. He ended the war with forty victories, making him the highest-scoring American pilot. In December 1944 Bong was recalled to the United States for the last time, and became one of the first pilots to convert to Lockheed P-80 Shooting Star jet fighters. He was killed on 6 August 1945, when the P-80 he was flying crashed on take-off at Burbank, California.

8 Charles H. MacDonald— Lightning over Leyte

In the autumn of 1944 the Imperial Japanese forces in the Pacific found themselves in a desperate position, caught in the grip of a vast Allied pincer movement. From the south, advancing from Australia, came the American and Commonwealth forces of General Douglas MacArthur, while from the east, thrusting out from Pearl Harbor, came the US Pacific Fleet under Admiral Chester Nimitz, bearing with it the greatest concentration of naval firepower in history.

In October 1944, the jaws of the great pincer closed on the Philippines. The blow fell on the island of Leyte, in the centre of the island group, where the Japanese defences were weakest. Four American divisions went ashore in the east of the island, and for a time encountered only moderate resistance; then the Japanese decided to throw all their available resources into an attempt to hold Leyte and isolate the American troops there. In the weeks following 17 October, when the Americans invaded, they poured troops, equipment and aircraft into the island and despatched three naval task forces in support of the overall effort. The Japanese naval forces were defeated by the US Third Fleet in three major actions, known collectively as the Battle for Leyte Gulf; the enemy lost three battleships, one large and three small carriers, ten cruisers and many smaller craft, the surviving warships being harried mercilessly by American carrier aircraft as they withdrew.

Despite this setback, by the beginning of November the

Japanese had succeeded in bringing tens of thousands of reinforcements to Leyte through their base at Ormoc Bay, in
the north-west of the island, and MacArthur decided to land
a division there to assault the Japanese positions. The date
of the landing was fixed at 7 December 1944, and all American air units in the Leyte area were called upon to afford
maximum support; the Japanese Air Force was certain to
resist the invasion with every available means.

As well as the naval aircraft of the carrier task forces operating around Leyte, the Americans had at their disposal
several fighter groups of the us Fifth Air Force, which had
established themselves on hastily-prepared strips in the east
of the island. They included the 49th and 475th Fighter
Groups, commanded respectively by Colonel Gerald Johnson and Colonel Charles E. MacDonald, both of them already high-scoring pilots.

Tall and stern-faced, MacDonald was a career officer in
the USAAF, a man for whom split-second decision was second
nature. He had fought his way through the great American
retreat from the Pacific in 1942, and during the battles of
1943 he had begun to achieve success as a fighter pilot and a
superb leader, both in the air and on the ground. In combat
he was aggressive, a trait that was demonstrated during a
fighter escort mission to Rabaul in 1943. *En route* to the objective with the bombers, a group of B-26 Marauders, the
formation encountered severe weather and the mission was
aborted. The bombers, however, failed to receive the radio
recall and pressed on towards the target. Most of the escorting fighters turned back—all except MacDonald and seven
other pilots. At the head of the depleted fighter formation
MacDonald climbed flat out to 20,000 feet and the seven
fighters fanned out ahead of the bombers, a move designed
to give the enemy the impression that more fighters were
following. The Japanese attacked over Cape Gazelle and for
the best part of an hour MacDonald and his colleagues
fought against overwhelming odds, enabling the bombers to

battle their way to the target and out again. MacDonald himself shot down two Zeros.

The summer of 1944 found him with fifteen victories and commanding officer of the 475th Group, whose three squadrons were equipped with twin-engined, twin-tailed Lockheed P-38 Lightnings. Although less manoeuvrable than single-engined types such as the Mustang and Thunderbolt, the Lightning possessed considerable range and speed and packed a powerful punch in the shape of one 20-mm cannon and four machine-guns, grouped in the nose. Moreover, its twin engines made it ideal for long-range flying over the ocean, and it became a firm favourite with pilots in the Pacific Theatre. In April 1944 it was a squadron of Lightnings, operating at the extremity of their range from Guadalcanal, that caught and shot down the aircraft carrying Admiral Isoroku Yamamoto, Commander-in-Chief of the Imperial Japanese Navy, who was on his way to Rabaul.

In the summer of 1944 the 475th Group pioneered a variety of techniques designed to increase the Lightning's range still further, and during this period Charles Lindbergh, of Atlantic crossing fame, flew with the Group to teach its pilots long-range cruise control procedures. The pilots learned much from the 'Old Pro', who once or twice became the target for some good-natured leg-pulling. On one occasion, while flying with a Lightning formation, Lindbergh radioed to say that he was having trouble in keeping up with the rest. A laconic voice answered him: 'Hey, Lindy, that ain't the Spirit of St Louis you're flying. Get your gear up.' An embarrassed Lindbergh immediately retracted his undercarriage, which he had forgotten all about.

The 475th Group, and Charles MacDonald, returned to the Philippines in October 1944, setting up base at Dulag airstrip on Leyte. Some distance up the road to the north was Gerry Johnson's 49th Group, on another primitive strip. Conditions were far from good; both strips became seas of stinking mud after every rain, and personnel lived and worked in makeshift lean-to structures covered in tent canvas that only kept out some of the water. The 475th Group's part in the landing by the US 77th Division at Ormoc Bay involved the provision of close fighter cover for the convoy on the way in. Of the 475th's three squadrons, the 431st and 432nd—with MacDonald flying with the latter—would fly low on the flanks of the invasion force, while the 433rd would fly top cover several thousand feet higher up. Meanwhile, the three squadrons of Johnson's 49th Group were to sweep further afield in an endeavour to stop Japanese aircraft getting through to the convoy. Each group was to put thirty six Lightnings into the air initially, with sufficient reserves to maintain continual air cover.

Take-off was scheduled for first light on 7 December. To wait any longer would be to risk being strafed by Japanese aircraft. MacDonald was the first to take off, his silver Lightning with the yellow spinners—nicknamed Putt-Putt-Maru—lifting cleanly from the pitted surface of Dulag's runway. As he began a gentle climb to 6,000 feet the other P-38s of the 432nd Squadron dropped into place behind him. After the 432nd came the 431st, led by Major Tommy McGuire—the Group's highest-scoring pilot, with over thirty victories already to his credit. Now that Bob Johnson had gone home from the European Theatre, McGuire was the closest rival to Richard Bong, who was still active in the Pacific.

McGuire had originally been assigned to the 49th Fighter Group in August 1943, but had transferred to the 475th shortly afterwards. In his first air combat over Wewak he had shot down three enemy aircraft, an achievement he was to repeat on no fewer than five occasions; on five other occasions he destroyed two. But on this December day in 1944, it would be Charles MacDonald, and not McGuire, who would capture the limelight. Forty miles out from Dulag the 475th's pilots sighted the convoy: a great armada of ships, its flanks patrolled by destroyers. The Lightning squadrons moved to their stations and weaved across the sky over the vessels, alert for the first signs of trouble. MacDonald dropped his eyes from the horizon for a second to scan his instruments, and saw to his dismay that for some inexplicable reason his fuel gauges were showing his P-38's tanks to be only a quarter full. He had no alternative but to hand over command of the 432nd to the senior flight leader, Captain Perry Dahl, and return to Dulag to refuel. While he was still on the ground the other Lightnings began to come back in ones and twos—sure sign that there had been a fight. MacDonald learned that there had been a skirmish with some Zeros soon after he turned for base, and that Dahl had been shot down. (Dahl, in fact, managed to bale out with a slight head wound and came down in Ormoc Bay, where he floated in his dinghy until nightfall. After dark he paddled ashore and hid in the jungle, where he was later picked up by Filipino partisans. They smuggled him out of Japanese territory and he turned up at Dulag a fortnight later.)

As soon as the Lightnings were refuelled they took off once more for Ormoc Bay. At 11.20 they sighted the ships, and a few seconds later one of the pilots reported three aircraft, ahead and above. They were quickly identified as enemies: tubby single-engined Mitsubishi Raiders, known by the Allied code-name of 'Jack'.

MacDonald pushed his throttles wide open and climbed towards the enemy, who immediately turned away and split up. MacDonald selected the middle aircraft and followed it into the top of a cumulus cloud, his wingman following at a distance of half a mile. Bursting out into sunlight once more, the American saw his target turning hard right and curved round to cut him off. The Japanese pilot immediately reversed the turn and plunged into the sheltering cloud once more. The cat-and-mouse game went on for five minutes; every time the Japanese broke cloud cover he found MacDonald behind him, anticipating his every move and always a little closer.

With the range down to 150 yards, MacDonald opened fire. His shells and bullets chewed up the Jack from nose to tail and the propeller turned more slowly until it stopped altogether. The enemy fighter flicked into a fast spin and the pilot baled out.

Away to the right a second Jack was going down in flames, torn apart by the gunfire of MacDonald's wingman, Lieutenant-Colonel Meryl Smith. Then, suddenly, the smoke trails of tracer bullets enmeshed MacDonald's Lightning; the fire came from the third Jack, which had crept up on his tail unobserved. MacDonald broke hard and turned to meet the Jack, but the enemy pilot turned inside him and more bullets flashed past the Lightning's tail, dangerously close. MacDonald was sweating; try as he might, he could not out-turn the enemy.

Suddenly, the Jack shuddered as though a giant hammer had struck it. Fragments tore away from it and it spiralled down, streaming white smoke. A Lightning slid into place off MacDonald's wingtip; it was Smith, who had seen what was happening and come to the rescue. Together, the two P-38s resumed their patrol over the convoy; no further enemy aircraft appeared and they returned to base to refuel and rearm, landing at 12.15. An hour and fifteen minutes later MacDonald was airborne again, leading a section of four Lightnings. Once again, all was quiet over the American ships; the scene below was almost peaceful, with landing craft ferrying men and equipment to the beach-head.

MacDonald decided to scout to the west, where Japanese vessels had been reported. The Lightnings cruised over the sea at 4,000 feet, their pilots searching the horizon for the enemy ships. Suddenly, there was a warning shout over the R/T; eight enemy fighters were diving fast from astern. The Americans broke and split up, turning hard in the hope of getting on the Japs' tails as their high speed carried them past. A Zero flashed by MacDonald's nose and he got in a short deflection burst. It was a lucky shot; the burst hit the enemy fighter just behind the cockpit, in the vulnerable spot where the tail was joined to the forward fuselage and wings, which were assembled in one piece, and the Zero fell apart. MacDonald glimpsed the debris plunging into the sea.

A few hundred yards away a Lightning was twisting and turning in a desperate attempt to elude a Zero, which clung to its tail and fired in short, accurate bursts. MacDonald closed in on the enemy fighter, whose pilot had not seen him, and opened fire when the Zero filled his sights. The Japanese fighter streamed white smoke and disintegrated. It was all over in a matter of seconds. MacDonald looked round for the other Lightning, but there was no sign of it.

There was no time to congratulate himself over his third victory of the day. A mile away, a lone Zero—apparently the sole survivor of the Japanese formation—was flying westwards at full throttle. MacDonald went in hot pursuit, together with two other Lightnings, and rapidly caught up with the enemy fighter. The Japanese pilot, knowing that he was unable to outrun the faster P-38, went into a tight turn through 360°—a manoeuvre that gained a little ground. Rolling out on a westerly heading once more he sped away, but in less than a minute the Lightnings had caught up with him again and forced him into another turn. With three against one, the outcome was inevitable. Concentrating on getting away from MacDonald, the Japanese pilot ran into a burst from Lieutenant Leo Blakely, flying the third P-38, who managed to cut across the enemy's turn. The Zero burst into flames and fell into the sea.

Two more Zeros appeared briefly and MacDonald turned towards them, but they escaped into a cumulus. Then he spotted a third Zero, low down and diving fast towards the American ships. The Lightnings followed it, but had to break off when a curtain of fire from the vessels' anti-aircraft guns spread across the sky. The Zero sped like an arrow through the inferno, heading straight for one of the ships. A moment later it collided with the vessel in a gout of smoke and flame. A new word had entered the terminology of the Pacific War: Kamikaze. . . .

The Lightnings turned for home, short of fuel. On arrival at Dulag MacDonald learned that Meryl Smith was missing and took off to search for him as soon as his aircraft was refuelled. He searched fruitlessly until dusk before returning to base with a heavy heart for the last time that day. Lt.-Col. Smith was never seen again.

Shortly afterwards, MacDonald had a call from the 49th Group; Gerry Johnson had also got three enemy aircraft in the space of as many minutes. Probing inland from Ormoc Bay, Johnson had spotted three Oscars—Nakajima Ki-43 fighters—below. 'There are three Oscars down below,' he had told his wingman. 'Count them, one, two, three.' Almost before the wingman had finished counting, the third Oscar was blazing among the trees.

The 475th Group's score for the day—the third anniversary of the Japanese attack on Pearl Harbor—was twenty-eight enemy aircraft destroyed. Tommy McGuire of the 431st Squadron had got two. A few days later, on 26 December, McGuire shot down four Zeros, bringing his score to thirty-eight—only two short of Dick Bong's total of forty.

On 7 January, 1945, McGuire was leading a patrol of four Lightnings on an offensive mission against the enemy airfield at Los Negros when a lone Zero was sighted. The Lightnings dived on the tail of the enemy, who waited until they were almost in range—then flung his aircraft into a tight left-handed turn that brought him on the tail of Lieutenant Rittmeyer, McGuire's wingman. A short burst, and Rittmeyer's P-38 went down in flames. The Zero turned easily inside the other three Lightnings, and in an effort to get at him McGuire committed one of flying's deadly sins: he attempted a tight turn at low speed. His P-38 plunged into the jungle; the other two Lightnings managed to get away.

Tommy McGuire was the first of the leading aces of the Leyte battle to die. Gerry Johnson followed him a few months later, killed in a flying accident. Charles MacDonald survived the war. At the end of hostilities he was the fifth highest-scoring American fighter ace with twenty-seven kills; he was awarded the Distinguished Service Cross twice and the Distinguished Flying Cross five times. He retired from the United States Air Force in the 1950s.

9 Adolf Galland—
Fighter General

Like a school of sharks, the six sleek Messerschmitt 262 fighters arrowed through the sky over the Danube, high over the ruins of Hitler's Third Reich. It was 26 April 1945, and the ring of steel was tightening remorselessly around the heart of Germany. Ahead of the advancing American, British and Russian armies, the Allied fighter-bombers roved at will, harrying the shattered remnants of the Wehrmacht and slaughtering what was left of the Luftwaffe on its few remaining airfields.

The Messerschmitt 262 jet fighter had been the Luftwaffe's great hope; a year earlier it could have wrought havoc among the formations of American daylight bombers, but its entry into service had been delayed by internal wrangling and now it had come too late. The missions its pilots flew, like that on this April day in the last fortnight of the war in Europe, were little more than futile gestures in the face of overwhelming odds.

Each of the six pilots who flew these 262s was well aware of the grim truth—the man who led the formation most of all. For General Adolf Galland had been one of the Luftwaffe's first combat pilots, and now he was one of the last. He had witnessed its heady climb to success in the early days only five years earlier, and now he was participating in its collapse.

Like so many other Luftwaffe pilots of his vintage, Galland had first taken to the air in a glider in the decade after

World War I, eventually going solo in 1928 shortly after his seventeenth birthday. Later, he learned to fly powered aircraft at one of the state-sponsored flying clubs, and in 1933—when Hitler came to power and the clubs were incorporated into the new military structure of the Third Reich— he was one of a group of young pilots selected to go to Italy for secret training. At the end of his course he qualified as a commercial pilot and was attached to Lufthansa, the German airline, flying on the regular European services. Finally, in 1934, he joined the ranks of the embryo and clandestine Luftwaffe, receiving his commission as a Second Lieutenant in October of that year after military training in Dresden. In April 1935 he was posted to the first fighter unit of the reborn Luftwaffe: No. 2 'Richthofen' Fighter Wing (*Jagdgeschwader 2*), named after the World War I ace. The unit was equipped with a mixture of Heinkel He 51 and Arado Ar 68 fighters, and Galland survived a serious crash in one of the latter.

In July 1936 the Spanish Civil War broke out, and both the Germans and Italians lost little time in sending men and equipment to Spain to serve General Franco's Nationalist cause. A few weeks later, the Soviet Union intervened in a similar manner on the Republican side. The initial German contribution consisted of aircraft and crews, and Luftwaffe personnel posted for a tour with the Condor Legion—as the contingent was known—reported to a secret office in Berlin where they were issued with civilian clothes, Spanish currency and papers. Then they left for Doberitz, where they joined a '*Kraft durch Freude*' (Strength through Joy) tour ostensibly bound for Genoa via Hamburg. Their real destination was El Ferrol, in north-west Spain.

By the beginning of 1937 the Condor Legion, commanded by Major-General Hugo Sperrle, consisted of three fighter squadrons, four bomber squadrons, a reconnaissance squadron and a seaplane squadron, as well as anti-aircraft batteries and support units. In May 1937 Galland arrived in Spain and joined No. 3 Squadron of *Jagdgruppe* J/88, flying Heinkel He 51 biplane fighters on the northern front. The other two squadrons were beginning to receive brand-new Messerschmitt 109s. As commander of the He 51 Squadron, Galland's task was to provide close support for the Nationalist ground forces. His pilots flew six or seven missions a day and wrought considerable havoc among the enemy troops. There were occasional brushes with Republican fighters, but the old He 51s were usually on the defensive and although some of Galland's colleagues scored victories he himself was not successful. His tour in Spain expired in July 1938, by which time he had flown 280 missions, and he was recalled to Germany just as his squadron was starting to re-equip with Messerschmitt 109s.

The next few months were spent behind a desk at the Air Ministry in Berlin, and it came as a considerable relief when, in the summer of 1939, Galland was ordered to form two new ground-attack units in readiness for the coming assault on Poland. During the twenty-seven days of the Polish campaign Galland flew fifty sorties in a Henschel Hs 123 ground-attack biplane, receiving the Iron Cross 2nd Class and promotion to captain for his efforts. All this time he had made ceaseless attempts to get himself transferred to fighters, and at the end of October 1939 he finally succeeded. He was posted to the 27th Fighter Wing (JG 27) at Krefeld, flying Messerschmitt 109s.

Although there was frequent skirmishing during the 'Phoney War' period between the Luftwaffe and Allied fighter squadrons over the Franco-German border, Krefeld was opposite neutral Holland and JG 27's pilots saw no action until May 1940, when the Germans launched their offensive in the west. JG 27 flew in support of the advance through Belgium, and it was over Liege on 12 May that Galland scored his first victory. Patrolling at 12,000 feet with the rest of his squadron, he sighted a formation of eight Belgian Hurricanes below and dived to the attack. The Belgians did not wake up to the danger until the 109s opened fire. Galland made two passes at a Hurricane and shot away its rudder. As it spiralled earthwards he attacked a second enemy fighter, which tried to escape by diving. Galland clung to it and opened fire at a range of 100 yards; the Hurricane stalled and dived vertically into the ground. Later that day, Galland shot down a third Hurricane over Tirlemont.

JG 27 leap-frogged from one advanced airstrip to another in the wake of the German *Blitzkrieg*. On 19 May it was at Charleville, in the foothills of the Ardennes; at dusk that day Galland shot down his fourth aircraft, a French Potez 63 reconnaissance machine. A few days later, during the evacuation of the British Expeditionary Force from Dunkirk, Galland encountered the Royal Air Force for the first time. While flying a sortie with JG 27's staff flight on 29 May the German pilot sighted a formation of Blenheim bombers and ordered an attack. He fastened himself to the tail of one Blenheim, which took violent evasive action, but his bullets found their mark and the bomber crashed into the sea.

The following day, JG 27 was bounced over Dunkirk by a squadron of Spitfires. Galland, who was flying No. 2 to JG 27's co, Colonel Ibel, shot down one of the British fighters, but the Spitfires evened the score by shooting down Ibel, who crash-landed and walked back to base.

On 3 June, JG 27 was one of the fighter units detailed to escort a large formation of German bombers in an attack on airfields and installations in the Paris area. The French put all their available fighters into the air and fierce dogfights flared up. Galland shot down a Curtiss Hawk, then his squadron was attacked by 20 Morane 406s. Galland fired at one from point-blank range, approaching so close that his propeller struck the Morane's wing as the French fighter burst into flames. As he turned away, Galland loosed off a short burst at a second Morane, which went down trailing smoke, but he did not see it crash and could only claim a 'probable'.

At the end of the French campaign, by which time he had scored thirteen victories, Galland was transferred to the 'Schlageter' Geschwader, JG 26, which was stationed at Guines on the Channel coast. On 24 July he saw action over England for the first time when Spitfires were encountered during a sweep over the Thames Estuary. Galland shot one down, but two of JG 26's aircraft failed to return. 'We were no longer in any doubt,' Galland wrote later, 'that the RAF would prove a most formidable opponent.' During the next few weeks the pilots of JG 26 saw almost continual action over southern England. By 24 September Galland's personal score had risen to forty aircraft destroyed, and he was summoned to Berlin to receive the Oak Leaves to the Knight's Cross from Hitler. It was a moving moment, tarnished only by the fact that Galland and his fellow pilots now knew beyond all doubt that the Battle of Britain had been lost.

At the beginning of 1941, following a short rest in Germany, Galland's JG 26 was sent to Brittany and given the task of protecting German warships in Brest harbour and the U-boat pens on the French coast, which were then under construction. Apart from an occasional skirmish with Spitfires and the shooting down of one or two RAF reconnaissance aircraft, the first weeks of 1941 passed quietly enough; the greatest excitement came on 10 May, when JG 26 was suddenly ordered off the ground after dark to intercept the Messerschmitt 110 flown by Rudolf Hess, Hitler's deputy, who was defecting to Britain. Realizing the hopelessness of the task, and believing that Hess would not have enough fuel to reach his destination, Galland ordered up only a few aircraft, which returned without sighting anything. Later, to everyone's surprise, it was learned that Hess had reached Scotland.

On 22 June 1941 German forces invaded Russia, and with the transfer of many Luftwaffe units to the eastern front JG

26 became one of only two fighter groups on the Channel coast. Both groups soon had their work cut out, for in the weeks following the start of the Russian campaign the RAF began to send out squadrons of medium bombers, strongly escorted by fighters, to attack targets in north-west France.

During one of these attacks, on 21 June 1941, Galland had his first serious brush with death. Shortly after noon, JG 26 took off to intercept a formation of Blenheims attacking the German airfield at St Omer, escorted by about fifty Spitfires and Hurricanes. The Messerschmitts took the British by surprise, coming down in a long dive from 10,000 feet and breaking through the fighter escort. Galland eased out of his dive on the tail of a Blenheim and opened fire; the bomber burst into flames immediately and went down to crash near the perimeter of St Omer, some of the crew baling out.

Galland turned on a second Blenheim, firing in short bursts until black smoke streamed back from its starboard engine and it nosed down. He saw the crew jump, confirming a certain kill even though he did not see the Blenheim crash. The next instant the Spitfires were upon him; tracer bullets streamed past his cockpit and he threw his 109 into a series of violent evasive manoeuvres, but the enemy fire had struck home in his radiator and a few moments later his engine seized. By good fortune he was over Calais-Marck airfield and managed to make a forced landing there. A light aircraft from JG 26's field picked him up half an hour later.

He was airborne again later that afternoon, engaging Spitfires over Boulogne. He shot down one of them—his seventieth victory—and was so intent on following it down to confirm its crash that he failed to see another Spitfire on his tail. The first inkling of its presence came when bullets ripped into his fighter, tearing away the right side of the fuselage and sending splinters into his arm and head. The Spitfire disappeared and Galland turned towards home, cau-

tiously checking the controls. His altitude was 18,000 feet—
sufficient in theory to allow him to glide in.

Suddenly the Messerschmitt's fuel tank exploded sending
streams of burning petrol into the cockpit. Desperately,
spurred on by the horror of being burned alive, he undid his
safety harness and pushed at the cockpit canopy. It was stuck
fast. He pushed again, with all his strength, and after long
seconds the canopy came free and whirled away in the slipstream. He pulled back the stick and then jerked it forward,
hoping to be thrown from the cockpit, but his parachute got
stuck against the fixed part of the canopy. He dangled half
in and half out of the blazing 109, one arm round the aerial
mast and the other tugging frantically at the parachute. The
earth whirled crazily up to meet him. Then, abruptly, he
was falling through space, away from the heat and the
flames. He was so relieved that he almost forgot to pull the
ripcord. He landed heavily but safely in the Forest of Boulogne, and after having his wounds treated in a nearby naval
hospital he was back with his unit by nightfall.

After this incident Galland was grounded on the orders of
the Luftwaffe High Command, although he did fly frequently on non-operational sorties. While returning from
one of these—an air test—one day in July he encountered a
formation of Blenheims and Spitfires attacking St Omer; it
seemed too good an opportunity to miss. Joining up with
other Messerschmitts of his group he swept down through
the Spitfire escort, closing in on a Blenheim and setting the
bomber's starboard engine on fire. Once again, intent on the
fate of his victim, he neglected to look behind; a cannon
shell shattered his cockpit, wounding him in the head, and it
was only with extreme difficulty that he managed to shake
off his pursuer and regain his base. Only the day before, his
senior rigger had fitted extra armour plate to the cockpit
canopy of his 109, and it was this that the shell had struck.
Without it, Galland's head would have been blown off. The
rigger got special leave and a gift of one hundred Marks.

Galland continued to lead JG 26 in action through the summer and autumn of 1941, but there were greater things in store for him. In November of that year Werner Mölders, at that time Germany's greatest fighter ace, was killed in an air crash, and Galland was appointed to succeed him as *General der Jagdflieger* (General of the Fighter Arm). This staff post carried a considerable weight of authority and elevated Galland to the top of the chain of command in all matters pertaining to Luftwaffe fighter operations, responsible directly to Göring and Hitler. Soon after his appointment, he had to face a stern test: the co-ordination of all Luftwaffe fighter units on the Atlantic coast, in strict secrecy, to provide full air cover for Operation Thunderbolt— the breakout of the battle cruisers Scharnhorst, Gneisenau and Prinz Eugen from the French port of Brest and their subsequent dash through the Channel to northern Germany. In the event the German fighter pilots excelled in their task, and the warships got through the Channel despite determined attacks by the RAF and the Fleet Air Arm.

During most of 1942 Galland was employed mainly on inspection tours of Luftwaffe fighter units in Italy, North Africa and the Soviet Union. At the end of the year he was appointed Major-General—the youngest officer of this rank in the German forces, at the age of thirty. By this time the principal cities of Germany were beginning to suffer increasingly heavy attacks by the night raiders of RAF Bomber Command, and the first squadrons of the United States Eighth Air Force to arrive in England had begun to make probing attacks by daylight on 'fringe' targets round the western frontier of the Reich. It was clear to Galland that 1943 would be a decisive year, and that if the enemy bombers were to be mastered all the resources of the German aircraft industry must be geared up to full production of fighter aircraft. His theories soon brought him into open conflict with Göring who, together with Hitler, believed that priority should be given to new bombers and attack aircraft.

The internal struggle became even more bitter in the summer of 1943, when—with the Allied strategic air offensive against Germany well under way—Hitler decreed that the Luftwaffe's main effort in the west should be devoted to 'reprisal' raids on British targets.

In the autumn of 1943, Galland decided that the time had come for him to gain some first-hand experience of operations against the American daylight bombers. Attaching himself against orders to a fighter group, he took off in a Focke-Wulf 190 one morning to intercept an American raid on an aircraft factory at Marienburg. He succeeded in shooting down a B-17, but he returned to base a seriously disturbed man. For the first time, he realized the frailty of the Luftwaffe's fighter effort against the weight of firepower the Allies were sending against Germany day after day. On this occasion the raid had been between 200 and 300 strong, and there had been no fighter escort. Even so, the German fighter attacks had been far from determined in the face of the heavy American defensive fire. What would it be like, Galland wondered, when swarms of long-range fighters accompanied the Fortresses and Liberators on every trip?

Although the Luftwaffe enjoyed some notable successes against the daylight bombers—such as during the raid on Schweinfurt on 14 October 1943, when 60 B-17s were destroyed and 138 damaged—German fighter losses continued to mount and the bombers inflicted more and more devastation on their targets, for which Göring laid the blame squarely on the German fighter arm. Seething at the injustice, Galland fought back against his chief's accusations and stormy meetings between the two became commonplace. On one occasion, when Göring suggested that some fighter pilots had gained their Iron Crosses by faking their combat reports, Galland hurled his own decoration on the *Reichsmarschall*'s desk and refused to wear any medals for six months afterwards.

Galland continued to fly in combat whenever the opportu-

nity arose, and in the spring of 1944 he had his first unnerv-
ing experience of American long-range fighters. Together
with Johannes Trautloft, another fighter ace, he took off to
intercept a huge force of enemy bombers on their way to
Berlin. Two pilots came upon a straggling B-17 and Galland
shot it down, Trautloft having turned for home with
jammed guns. Then a flight of Mustangs pounced, and Galland found himself fleeing for his life. He extracted every
last ounce of power out of his Focke-Wulf, but he was unable to shake off his pursuers and bullets streamed past his
aircraft, unpleasantly close. In desperation, he employed an
old trick that had saved his life once before, during the Battle of Britain; he fired off everything he had into the open
air ahead of him. Grey smoke trails from his guns streamed
back towards the Mustangs who broke away violently in
surprise. Galland, making full use of the precious seconds he
had gained, managed to get away.

In the months that followed the Allied invasion of
Europe, Galland's frustration—and outspokenness—increased
beyond toleration level as he watched the Luftwaffe's
fighter units being wasted on the western front, where the
Allies enjoyed complete superiority, instead of being hus-
banded for the air defence of Germany. The last straw
finally came on 1 January 1945, when nearly three hundred
German fighters were sacrificed in a desperate low-level attack on Allied airfields in France and Belgium, timed to co-
incide with the German offensive in the Ardennes. Galland's opposition to this attack led to his dismissal from the
post of *General der Flieger;* his fall from grace was complete.

Nevertheless, his prowess as a pilot and fighter leader was
not in dispute, and in January 1945 Hitler ordered him to
form a new fighter unit equipped with the Luftwaffe's for-
lorn hope: the Messerschmitt 262 jet, in the operational de-
velopment of which he had already had a hand. The nucleus
of the new unit—*Jagdverband* (JV) 44—was formed at Bran-

denburg-Briest on 10 February 1945. By the beginning of March Galland had recruited forty-five fighter pilots, all of them highly experienced. There were twelve of the Luftwaffe's leading aces, including one Lieutenant-General, two Colonels, a Lieutenant-Colonel, three Majors and five Captains, ten of them holders of the Knight's Cross.

In the middle of March JV 44, with its full complement of Me 262s, moved to München-Riem, which was to be its main base of operations during March and April. Its main targets were the bombers of the US 15th Air Force, coming up from the south. Operational flying was a nightmare, with the Allies subjecting the 262s' bases to almost daily attacks and marauding fighter-bombers lurking on the approaches to the airfields in the hope of catching the jets during their vulnerable landing phase. In the air, however, the 262s were unmatched. During the last weeks of the war Galland's units received stocks of R4M 5-cm air-to-air rockets; each 262 could carry twenty-four and the effect of a salvo on a bomber formation was devastating. Galland himself shot down two B-26 Marauders in a single firing-pass with his rockets on 15 April, and claimed two more with his 30-mm cannon during the mission over the Danube on 26 April. This brought his total number of kills to 103. Towards the end of this sortie he was 'bounced' by Mustangs and his 262 was badly hit; he staggered back to Riem and made an emergency landing in the middle of an enemy air attack. Adolf Galland's combat career ended there, cowering miserably in a bomb crater beside his shattered jet while Thunderbolts turned the airfield's installations into burning wreckage.

A few days later, the surviving 262s were evacuated to Salzburg. They were still there on 3 May, when tanks of the United States Seventh Army rolled on to the airfield.

10 Erich Hartmann— Ace of Aces

It was the young German fighter pilot's first taste of action. Just a few minutes earlier he had taken off in a cloud of dust from the airfield at Soldatskaya, in the Caucasus, to patrol the line of the Terek River. He had been flying as wingman to one of his squadron's most experienced pilots, and he had felt confident enough—but now his leader had vanished and he was fighting for his life.

The two Messerschmitt 109s had dived on a pair of Soviet Ilyushin Il-2 ground-attack aircraft. It should have been an easy kill—but the inexperienced young pilot had missed his target badly, and as he climbed steeply away to make a second attempt the Russian fighters which had been escorting the Ilyushins suddenly pounced. Desperately, the German pilot dived for the shelter of a layer of cloud. As he broke through it, he snatched a hasty glance over his shoulder and saw another aircraft racing after him. He was completely alone; there was no sign of his leader, and he panicked. At full throttle he hurtled westwards, with no idea of his true position, curled into a sweating ball in the cockpit and expecting to feel the shudder of cannon shells at any moment. A minute later, he risked another glance rearwards—and almost passed out with relief. His pursuer had vanished.

Then another crisis arose: the red fuel warning light on his instrument panel began to blink. Five minutes later, the Messerschmitt's engine stopped dead. The young pilot made a successful belly-landing next to a German convoy twenty

miles short of his base, eventually arriving back in an army car. A stormy reception awaited him. The first thing he discovered was that the 'enemy' fighter which had pursued him had in fact been his leader, who had been frantically trying to contact him by radio. Mistaking his leader's 109 for a Russian fighter was only one of his sins; icily, his squadron commander ticked off the others. He had, it was forcefully pointed out, separated from his leader without orders; flown into his leader's firing position; dived through the cloud layer with no knowledge of what was underneath; failed to comply with his leader's instructions to rejoin; got lost; and, finally, written off his aircraft without having damaged the enemy.

For twenty-year-old Second Lieutenant Erich Hartmann, would-be fighter pilot newly arrived on the Russian front, it was a dismal beginning. Yet in just two and a half short years, this same young man was to rise to a pinnacle of fame as the top fighter pilot of any nation; an all-time ace of aces, with 352 shot-down enemy aircraft to his credit . . .

The dust of the Caucasus was a long way from the picturesque town of Weissach, where Erich Hartmann was born on 19 April 1922. Nevertheless, he was no stranger to long journeys. As a child of three his father—a doctor—had taken the Hartmann family to Shanghai, where he had held a practice for several years. By 1929, however, civil unrest in China had reached such a pitch that the family returned to Germany for safety's sake, and made a new home at Weil im Schönbruch.

There was a flying club at an airfield near Stuttgart, a few miles away. Erich's mother, who had always had a taste for adventure, learned to fly there and in 1930 bought a share in a little Klemm two-seater. She would take her two sons flying almost every Sunday afternoon, and it came as a bitter blow to air-minded Erich when the economic collapse of 1932 forced them to sell the machine.

In 1933 Adolf Hitler came to power, and under the auspi-

ces of the Nazi Party a rash of flying and gliding clubs
sprang up all over Germany. In 1936 Erich's mother formed
a gliding club at Weil, and by the end of 1937 Erich—having
successfully qualified as a glider pilot—became an instructor
in the Glider Group of the Hitler Youth. His academic career, meanwhile, followed varying fortunes. He was not
happy in his first secondary school—a forbidding academy in
Rottweil, where the staff adhered strictly to national so-
cialist principles and were completely regimented. His father, a discerning man, noticed his son's discomfort and
quickly moved Erich and his younger brother, Alfred, to the
friendlier atmosphere of a grammar school near Stuttgart. It
was during his time at this school that Erich met Ursula
Paetsch, an attractive dark-haired teenager who was later to
become his wife.

Erich graduated from high school in April 1940, shortly
after his eighteenth birthday. The Germans had just invaded Norway and the *Blitzkrieg* in France and the Low
Countries was in the offing; it was a time when the youth of
Germany, confident of victory, was volunteering *en masse*
for the armed forces. Erich immediately applied to join the
Luftwaffe, and in October 1940 he joined Air Force Military
Training Regiment 10 at Neukuhren, in East Prussia. After
several weeks of gruelling basic training he was posted to
Berlin-Gatow, where he took to the air for the first time in a
military aircraft on 5 March 1941. He went solo just three
weeks later, completing his basic flying training the following October. Then came an advanced flying course, after
which he was posted to the Fighter School at Zerbst, near
Magdeburg, where he learned to fly the aircraft every young
would-be Luftwaffe pilot dreamed of: the Messerschmitt
109 fighter.

Despite the fact that he was a natural shot and achieved
high marks in air gunnery, Erich found the course at Zerbst
a tough one and it was with considerable relief that, at the
end of March 1942, he was awarded his coveted 'wings' and

a commission as Second Lieutenant. This was a dangerous point in his career, for his natural exuberance bred over-confidence and it was almost his undoing. In August 1942, while attending an advanced gunnery course at Gleiwitz, he flew down to Zerbst and beat up the airfield with a wild aerobatic sequence, then flew back to Gleiwitz and repeated the performance. As soon as he landed he was arrested and confined to his room for a week. It gave him plenty of time for thought—and, ironically, it saved his life. On the after-noon of his arrest someone else substituted for him and took up the aircraft he had been flying; the machine crashed and the pilot was killed.

At the end of his course Hartmann found to his delight that he had been posted to the élite No. 52 Fighter Wing (JG 52) which was operating on the Russian Front. A cou-ple of days later he reported to the Luftwaffe supply base at Cracow, in Poland, where he hoped to collect a new Messerschmitt 109 and ferry it to JG 52's base at Maikop, in the Caucasus. However, no 109s were available, so instead he offered to fly a Junkers 87 Stuka dive-bomber. He had never flown a Stuka before, but he reasoned that one aero-plane was much the same as another and he began to taxi out for take-off. As he approached the end of the runway, he found to his horror that the Stuka began to swing to the right—heading straight for the runway controller's wooden hut. Frantically he stamped on the rudder bar and brakes, all to no effect. A moment later the Stuka ploughed into the hut, reducing it to matchwood with its whirling propeller. The controller crawled out of the wreckage, shaking his fist at the crestfallen young pilot. Hartmann completed his jour-ney to Maikop on a hard bench in the vibrating fuselage of a Junkers 52 transport, flown by someone else.

From Maikop Hartmann was sent to join JG 52's Third Squadron (III/JG 52) at Soldatskaya, a little airstrip near the Terek River, north of the Caucasus Mountains. There, he was assigned to fly No. 2 to Warrant Officer Eduard

Rossmann, an experienced pilot with 80 victories already to his credit.

His first combat mission on 14 October 1942, when he did everything wrong, was hardly calculated to increase his stature in Rossmann's eyes. During his three-day penance, working with the ground crews, he resolved never to make the same mistakes again. During subsequent missions with Rossmann he took careful note of the other pilot's actions, saw the way in which he planned each attack carefully—with the maximum element of surprise and speed—and gradually began to realize how Rossmann was accumulating so many kills without taking punishment himself. He began to wonder how he could improve on Rossmann's tactics, and spent long hours planning his own theoretical methods of attack.

His chance to put his ideas into practice came on 5 November 1942, when he took off with three other 109s to intercept eighteen Il-2s escorted by ten Lagg-3 fighters. Tearing through the fighter screen, Erich and his leader raced after the Ilyushins, which were flying at low level. Selecting the Russian bomber on the far left of the formation, Hartmann closed right into one hundred yards before opening fire. His bullets and cannon shells bounced off the heavily-armoured Russian aircraft and he came round for another attempt. This time he managed to get underneath the Il-2 and fired a long burst into the bomber's vulnerable belly from a range of only two hundred feet. The enemy aircraft burst into flames and debris whirled back from it, striking Erich's fighter. As the Il-2 ploughed into the ground there was a muffled explosion and smoke streamed back from the 109's engine. With his fighter in flames Hartmann managed to pull off a successful forced landing just behind the German lines. For a second time he returned to his unit in an army vehicle—this time exulting over his first victory.

This battle convinced Hartmann that there was only one way to knock down his opponents consistently: get in as

close as possible and fire from point-blank range. Using
these tactics, he destroyed four more enemy aircraft by the
end of March 1943, and two months later his score had risen
to seventeen. The fight in which he claimed his seventeenth
victim, on 25 May, was very nearly his last; he was climbing
away after shooting down an La-9 fighter when, blinded by
the sun, he collided with another enemy aircraft and only
just managed to nurse his crippled fighter over the lines before making a forced landing. After that he was sent back to
Germany for a brief rest, returning to the front in July. His
return to combat was marked by a series of incredible leaps
in his score; on the 5th he shot down four more Russian aircraft, and two days later he destroyed seven in the course of
a series of hectic air fights.

By 3 August 1943 he had fifty confirmed victories. He was
now flying up to four sorties a day, and with the Russians on
the offensive on most sectors of the front action was not
hard to find. On 5 August his score stood at sixty, ten more
Russian aircraft having gone down before his guns, and two
weeks later he had equalled the score of the World War I
ace, Manfred von Richthofen, with eighty kills. By the end
of October his tally stood at one hundred and forty-eight, an
achievement that won him the award of the Knight's Cross
of the Iron Cross. Two years earlier, fifty victories would
have been sufficient to bring him a similar honour; but times
had changed, and now decorations came harder to Germany's fighting men.

His victories during the long summer of 1943 were accompanied by their share of close shaves. The closest of all came
on 19 August, when the squadron—now stationed in the
Donets Basin—was ordered to take off in support of the German ground forces, threatened with encirclement following
a major Russian breakthrough. Over the front line the
Messerschmitts encountered forty Il-2s, escorted by as many
fighters, and a fierce battle developed. Erich shot down a
pair of Il-2s, but then his own aircraft was hit and he was

compelled to make yet another forced landing. As he was climbing from the cockpit, he was relieved to see a German truck approaching. The relief, however, was short-lived—for the soldiers that jumped from the vehicle were Russians.

Hartmann, clutching his stomach and pretending to be wounded, was taken to the Russian HQ in a nearby village. Some time later he was placed on a truck which set off eastwards, deeper into Russian territory. The German was accompanied by two Russian soldiers, one driving, the other sitting in the back with him. Suddenly, a flight of German aircraft swept overhead and the driver braked sharply, ready to jump from the vehicle and take cover. Hartmann seized his chance. Bounding to his feet he struck his Russian guard a crippling blow in the stomach and leaped over the tailboard, running for his life through a field of tall sunflowers. He ran harder than he had ever run before, pursued by sporadic rifle fire. After five minutes he stumbled into a small valley and threw himself full length on the grass, gasping for breath.

After a while he got up and started to walk westwards, but the whole area was crawling with Russians and he returned to his valley, resolving to wait until nightfall before attempting to reach the German lines. As soon as darkness descended he set off. After a few minutes he sighted a Russian patrol and followed it, reasoning that it was probably heading for the German lines. Eventually, the Russians came to a hill and began to climb the slope. A few yards from the summit they were greeted by intense small-arms fire and scattered wildly.

As the enemy disappeared Hartmann ran up the hill towards the German positions, shouting in his own language. As he topped the rise, a bitter disappointment awaited him: all he found were a few cartridge cases. The German troops had melted away into the night. He started walking westwards again, and for two hours he stumbled across country. Suddenly, a challenge rang out through the darkness, accompanied by a shot. A bullet snicked through his trouser leg. A minute later he was seized and bundled roughly into a foxhole, where a suspicious German officer interrogated him. He had only just established his identity when the Russians attacked. Hartmann found himself with a rifle in his hand, firing into the darkness until the enemy assault melted away. It was the most terrifying experience of his career. The next day he returned to his squadron, much chastened by what he had undergone. One of his colleagues recalled later: 'He had lived through an experience very few of our men survived. It seemed to me that in these few harrowing hours he had grown much older.'

By the time Hartmann scored his 150th victory in the autumn of 1943 he had become a celebrity on both sides of the front line. His name was mentioned frequently in German propaganda broadcasts and his photograph appeared in the newspapers alongside those of other top-scoring pilots of JG 52. To the Russians he was 'Karaya One', his radio callsign with which they had become familiar; later they nicknamed him *Cherniye Chort*, or Black Devil, and offered a reward of 10,000 roubles to any pilot who shot him down.

Erich's Messerschmitt was adorned with a distinctive black design on its nose, and as soon as the Russians discovered that the pilot who flew this machine was one and the same with Karaya One and the Black Devil they became increasingly unwilling to engage him in combat. As a result Erich's score diminished during the winter of 1943 to such an extent that he had the black device painted out, making his 109 indistinguishable from any other. The improvement was immediate and dramatic; in January and February 1944 he scored a staggering total of fifty victories in a period of just sixty days.

His radio callsign, however, remained the same, and as a result the Russians always knew when he was airborne and made resolute efforts to eliminate him. On one day at the end of February 1944 he had a nerve-racking encounter

with a red-nosed Yak-9 fighter whose pilot seemed determined to ram him. After five minutes of frantic turning during which neither pilot was able to gain the advantage,
Erich managed to get below his opponent, who lost sight of
him. Seizing his advantage Hartmann pulled up sharply and
let the Russian have it from fifty feet. The Yak burned and
went down behind the German lines; the pilot baled out and
was captured by some soldiers. Later, Erich flew back to the
scene in a Fieseler Storch and picked up the man, a Captain,
who seemed only too happy to be alive. He remained as the
guest of JG 52 for two days before being sent back to a
prison camp in the rear.

By the summer of 1944 JG 52 was fighting against overwhelming odds, and the German pilots—still soldiering on in
their elderly Messerschmitts—were hard pressed to hold
their own against the latest types of fighter with which the
best Red Air Force units were now equipped. Nevertheless
Hartmann's score continued to grow steadily; it seemed that
he never returned from a mission without one or more
enemy aircraft to his credit. On one occasion, he destroyed
four Il-2s with a single burst. The bombers were flying in
tight echelon formation at low level and Hartmann fired at
the aircraft on the right, hitting it in the cockpit. The Il-2
rolled sharply to the left and the other three broke frantically to get out of its way. The weight of the bombs they
were carrying and their steep turns combined to make them
lose height; all four aircraft hit the ground and blew up.

On 2 March 1944 Hartmann destroyed no fewer than ten
enemy aircraft in a single day. Shortly afterwards he trav-
elled to Berchtesgaden to receive the coveted Oak Leaves
award from Hitler himself; this was followed by a brief spell
of leave. He returned to the front on 18 March to find his
unit based at Lwow in Poland, having leapfrogged rapidly
from base to base ahead of the Russian advance.

Another move followed in April—this time to Rumania,
where JG 52's task was to counter the raids on Rumanian

oilfields by large formations of American heavy bombers, escorted by long-range Mustang fighters. The Messerschmitts had no sooner settled in, however, than they were suddenly ordered back to the Crimea, where the Russians had launched yet another major offensive. During the next two months Erich's score reached two hundred and fifty, and between 20 July and 22 August 1944 he shot down another thirty-two machines. He was now running neck-and-neck with Major Gerd Barkhorn, the co of JG 52, who had been in action for a good deal longer than the younger pilot. Erich's big day came on 23 August, when he destroyed eight aircraft in the course of three missions; he had now passed Barkhorn and was the top-scoring fighter pilot of all time. Almost surreptitiously, his squadron colleagues began to lay bets as to whether Hartmann would reach the magic figure of three hundred; the tension grew noticeably as the days went by. It was not long before the suspense broke. Over the next twenty-four hours, in the course of a series of air battles, Hartmann accounted for ten more enemy aircraft. His three hundredth victim was an Airacobra—an American fighter supplied in quantity to the Russians on lend-lease—which he shot down in flames near Baranov. There was a tremendous party that night. . . .

Hartmann's superiors now felt that it was time for the ace to have a rest, and he was sent back to Germany. During his brief ten-day leave he received the Diamonds to the Knight's Cross, the highest decoration of Hitler's Germany, and married his Ursula. Then, all too soon, he was on his way back to rejoin his unit, now based in Czechoslovakia.

Now at last JG 52 had a chance to come to grips with the Americans. Erich's squadron was detached to Zilistea, in Rumania, and the pilots were airborne almost every day as the big formations of B-17s and B-24s cruised overhead, dragging their long vapour trails and with their guardian P-51 Mustangs weaving protectively among them. For Erich and his colleagues, used to low-level work against the Rus-

sians, there was something unreal about fighting at altitudes
in excess of 25,000 feet, tackling the great, glittering
bombers that droned on in their solid phalanes as though in-
viting the German fighters to attack them if they dared.

The Americans, however, quickly found that operations
over Rumania and Czechoslovakia could be a hazardous un-
dertaking—and not only the German fighters were responsible. On one occasion, just before the end of hostilities,
Erich's squadron was intercepting a formation of Russian
bombers in the Prague area and was about to go home, short
of fuel and ammunition, when a group of American Mustangs suddenly appeared and dived into the fray. It looked
like trouble for the German pilots—but a moment later they
watched in astonishment as the Mustangs and the escorting
Russian fighters turned furiously on one another; apparently
the Russians believed that the Mustangs had attacked them.
They were still shooting each other down in flames when the
Messerschmitts hurriedly left the scene.

The end of the war in Europe was close now. On 8 May
1945, the last day of hostilities, Erich took off for a last mission over Brno. Skirting the smoke cloud that rose from the
burning town he sighted a formation of Yak-11 fighters and
dived to attack. With his first pass he sent a Yak down in
flames, continuing his dive through the rest of the formation
and heading flat out for home. It was his 352nd, and last,
victim. Hours later came the German surrender. The personnel of JG 52 gave themselves up to an advance American armoured unit, but they were later handed over to the Russians, who meted out brutal treatment to them. For Erich
Hartmann, it was the start of a nightmare; he was to spend
ten fearful years in Soviet prison camps before eventually
being set free in 1955. Other prisoners, many of them
friends of his, were less fortunate; they never returned to
their homeland.

While Hartmann languished in Russia, other former
Luftwaffe fighter pilots of far less calibre reaped the re-

wards of their wartime exploits, cashing in on their memoirs. It seemed that the world's top-scoring pilot had been forgotten; his victories were frequently called into question by those who did remember and his claims often dismissed as ludicrous. Yet the fact remains that every one of those 352 kills was verified, either on film or by other pilots. It should also be remembered that the staggering totals of kills achieved by Luftwaffe pilots on the Eastern Front were made possible by two principal factors: the inexperience of the rank and file of Russian pilots (with the exception of the highly-trained Guards Fighter Regiments, which were excellent), and the fact that many German pilots served almost continuously in action against the Russians for four years, with only short leave breaks. For the vast majority of pilots, there was no such thing as a tour of operations, followed by the luxury of a rest and several months as an instructor with a flying school at the rear. The overall result was that as the skill of individual fighter pilots grew, the Russian Front became the 'happy hunting ground' of air fighting. To claim the destruction of six or eight enemy aircraft in a day might appear exorbitant—but similar successes were achieved by American pilots in the Pacific when the Japanese appeared in strength, which was not an everyday occurrence as it was in Russia.

Hartmann himself, today a senior officer in the West German Luftwaffe, offers this simple explanation for his overwhelming wartime success: 'I was afraid in the air of the big unknown factors. Clouds and sun were hate and love in my feeling world. Today I am sure that eighty per cent of my kills never knew I was there before I opened fire. My dogfights were fast and simple on that account. But one factor always worked for me more than any other. I found I could spot enemy planes long before my comrades—sometimes minutes before them. This was not experience and skill, but an advantage with which I was born. My rule for air fighting is this: *the pilot who sees the other first already has half the victory.*'

11 Werner Mölders— the Veteran

When Adolf Galland left the Condor Legion in Spain at the end of his tour in July 1938, his place as commanding officer of *Jagdgruppe* J.88's 3rd Squadron (III/J.88) was taken by a twenty-five-year-old officer named Werner Mölders, who at that time had been in Spain for three months flying Heinkel He 51s. So far, Mölders' experience of action had been limited to ground-attack work, for the He 51 was badly outclassed by the Russian-built fighters then in service with the Spanish Republican Air Force and as a matter of policy combat with them was avoided as far as possible. In the early part of 1938, fighter protection for the Heinkels was provided by Italian Fiats and the Messerschmitt 109Bs of J.88's 1st and 2nd Squadrons.

By July 1938, however, there were enough 109s in Spain to equip the whole of J.88, and that month Mölders' squadron received the first of its complement of brand-new Messerschmitt 109C-1s. It was while flying one of these machines, on 15 July 1938, that Mölders fought his first air combat.

While carrying out a patrol over the Northern Front, the pilots of III/J.88 encountered a strong formation of Russian I-16 fighters. Mölders soon got on the tail of one of them, but he was over-excited and opened fire while the range was still much too great. The I-16 escaped, but a few seconds later Mölders attacked another. This time there was no mistake; he closed right in and opened fire at point-blank range.

The enemy fighter burst into flames and crashed. It was Mölders' first victory—the first rung of the ladder which, in the course of a relatively short career, was to make his name a household word in his native Germany and earn the respect of his enemies. In years to come he never forgot his first air battle, or the mistakes he made while fighting it; later, many a young German pilot, going into action for the first time, was to owe his life to the advice Mölders gave him.

Strangely enough, this man whose expertise was soon to win him a permanent niche in aviation's hall of fame almost failed to become a pilot. Born on 18 March 1913, all he wanted from his early boyhood was to be a soldier. It was a desire that was strongly resisted by his mother, who had seen Werner's father—a schoolteacher by profession—swallowed up in the holocaust of World War I. She hoped fervently that Werner would change his mind, and so he did —but not in the way she would have wished. When he was ten an uncle took him for a flight, and from then on Werner had one ambition: he wanted to be a pilot.

In the years immediately after the First World War, however, Germany was forbidden to maintain an air force by the Treaty of Versailles, and it was as a soldier that Mölders began his military career, entering the Dresden Military Academy in 1932. By the time he passed out as a Second Lieutenant two years later, the wind of change had swept dramatically over Germany almost overnight; the Nazis had come to power and an embryo air force was being formed under conditions of the strictest secrecy.

Mölders lost no time in applying to join the new Service. After preliminary interviews he reported to a Luftwaffe selection centre, where he passed both written and medical examinations without difficulty. All that remained now was to get through the aptitude tests—and it was here that the problems started. He was shown into a room that was empty except for what looked like a dentist's chair. A medical officer told him to sit down in it, and immediately the chair began to revolve at high speed. When it finally stopped, the doctor told Mölders to get up—but the would-be pilot could hardly stand, and a few seconds later he was violently sick. It was not surprising that the authorities stamped 'rejected' on his application forms. A promising career might have ended there and then—but Mölders refused to be beaten. For the next month he subjected himself to endless physical exercises, making himself as fit as possible. Then he re-applied for assessment as aircrew, and although he experienced some nausea during the aptitude tests, he managed to control himself. This time, he was accepted.

The real test, however, was still to come. He began his flying training in March 1935, and every one of those early flights was a nightmare. He was continually airsick, and several times was on the point of being grounded—but each time he managed to convince his instructors that he would be all right if only he were allowed more time. Two things combined to save him: the fact that he had the makings of an excellent pilot, and his iron willpower. Gradually the attacks of giddiness became fewer, and by the time he graduated from flying school they had disappeared altogether.

Following the practice of most air forces, the Luftwaffe 'creamed off' the best of its young pilots to train as flying instructors, and after a short course on Junkers 52 transports Mölders was posted as an instructor to Wiesbaden, where he remained for two years. Then came his move to Spain in the spring of 1938. After his first victory in July his success rate grew at remarkable speed, and by the time his tour was ended in October he had destroyed fourteen enemy aircraft —making him the top-scoring Condor Legion pilot. More important than that was the experience he had gained in the science of air fighting—experience that was put to good use on his return to Germany. Together with other leading German pilots who had served in Spain, Mölders virtually rewrote the Luftwaffe's manual of fighter tactics, helping to devise the combat formations which, a few months later, were to prove far superior to any employed by the German Air Force's opponents.

The outbreak of World War II in September 1939 found Mölders in command of No. 1 Squadron, *Jagdgeschwader* 53 (I/JG 53), and it was not long before the unit was in action. On 20 September, after some cautious initial sparring, the Luftwaffe and the French Air Force joined battle in earnest over the Franco-German border. During the afternoon, six Curtiss Hawk fighters of the French *Groupe de Chasse* GC II/5 were escorting a reconnaissance aircraft over the front when the top flight of three French fighters was attacked by four Messerschmitt 109s of I/JG 53, led by Mölders. The Frenchmen broke wildly, but they were too late; Mölders got on the tail of a Curtiss and set it on fire with a short burst. The pilot baled out. In the air battle that followed a second Curtiss went down, while the French pilots accounted for a 109.

The next day, three Messerschmitts led by Mölders pounced on a luckless French Potez reconnaissance aircraft over Altheim. A very gallant French pilot in a Morane 406 fighter came to the Potez' rescue, but he was too late and the Messerschmitts attacked him in turn. Mölders allowed his two wingmen to get in the first bursts, then he closed in and gave the Morane the *coup de grâce* from point-blank range. The French pilot baled out, but his parachute failed to open.

The fighter pilots of JG 53 saw frequent action during the winter of 1939-40; to the airmen of both sides who battled over the frontier the term 'Phoney War' had little meaning. Allies and Germans alike knew that they were fighting the first round of the great test that was to come, and in the spring of 1940 the air battles flared up with renewed violence. By 10 May, Mölders' personal score stood at twenty-five enemy aircraft destroyed.

On that day the Germans launched their offensive in the

west, and in the three hectic weeks that followed Mölders went from victory to victory. He was already a national hero and decorations were showered on him—despite the fact that on more than one occasion he had been outspoken in his criticism of the Nazis. Werner Mölders was a devout Christian and a patriot; his allegiance was to his God and his country, and politics played no part in his makeup. His men worshipped him, bestowing the affectionate nickname of 'Daddy' on him. There was keen competition to fly in his squadron, not only because JG 53 was always in the forefront of the battle but also because there was an aura of invincibility about Mölders that made for excellent morale.

It was on 5 June, 1940—during the final phase of the Battle of France—that the myth of Mölders' invincibility was finally shattered. Shortly after five o'clock that afternoon, he was leading fifteen Messerschmitt 109s on a sweep at 25,000 feet over the Forest of Compiègne when eight French fighters—Dewoitine D.520s—were sighted at a lower altitude. The Germans dived through the French formation, shooting down two D.520s, and Mölders went after a third aircraft. This particular D.520, flown by Lieutenant Pomier-Layragues, took the German pilot completely by surprise. Instead of trying to escape by diving away, as Mölders had anticipated, he suddenly broke hard into a steep climbing turn and hurtled at the Messerschmitt head-on, firing as he came. As the French fighter sped overhead Mölders' aircraft was shaken by a series of vicious bangs: his windscreen shattered and smoke streamed back from his engine. Mölders wasted no time. He unfastened his safety harness, jettisoned the cockpit canopy and jumped. He landed safely, and as he was freeing himself from his parachute he was taken prisoner by some French artillerymen. Mölders at once asked if he might be allowed to meet the man who had shot him down, but he was too late. Even as the German parachuted down, Pomier-Layragues found himself engaged in a desperate single-handed fight against four more 109s.

He shot one of them down, but then six more German fighters joined the one-sided battle and the Frenchman's aircraft was torn apart by cannon-shells. Engulfed in flames, it went down and exploded among some houses. The pilot had not baled out.

Werner Mölders did not remain a prisoner for very long. In less than three weeks the Franco-German Armistice had been signed and he was released. In July 1940 he was promoted and given command of a Luftwaffe Fighter Wing— *Jagdgeschwader* 51—which was then building up its strength for the coming air offensive against Britain.

When Mölders was taken prisoner in France, his score— including his victories in Spain—stood at thirty-five. By the middle of October 1940 he had added a further twenty-four Spitfires and Hurricanes, bringing the total up to fifty-nine. The achievements of men such as Mölders, however, could not change the fact that the Royal Air Force had won the Battle of Britain; by the beginning of November the Luftwaffe's day-fighter operations had dwindled away to sorties across the Channel by small numbers of bomb-carrying Messerschmitts, or brief offensive sweeps over the south coast by up to a dozen aircraft. Mölders habitually led these sweeps himself, but during the second week in November he went down with a severe bout of influenza and placed his colleague and friend, *Oberleutnant* Claus, in temporary command. On the morning of 11 November, when the Messerschmitts returned from a sweep over the Thames estuary, Claus was not among them. Mölders was like a man demented; ill though he was, he insisted on taking off to look for his friend. For an age he flew back and forth low over the Channel just off the British coast, oblivious to the danger from RAF fighters, scanning the choppy water for a sign of a dinghy or lifejacket. He saw nothing; the English Channel, that great fighter pilots' graveyard of 1940, had claimed another victim.

Mölders and JG 51 remained in France until June 1941,

when the order came for a sudden move to Poland. A few days later, on 22 June, the Wehrmacht stormed into the Soviet Union.

For the Luftwaffe's fighter pilots, Russia during those summer weeks of 1941 was the killing ground. Their Russian opponents were totally unprepared and lacking experience, and the slaughter was fearful. The German pilots began to amass phenomenal scores, and Mölders was no exception. At the time his squadron left the western front his tally stood at eighty-two enemy aircraft destroyed—sixty-eight French and British, together with his fourteen Spanish victories— and now, in the space of just four weeks, he added thirty-three more, bringing his total up to a hundred and fifteen. Before long this score would be passed twice and even three times—but in the summer of 1941 it was considered incredible, the greatest achievement since von Richthofen's eighty victories in World War I.

The Luftwaffe High Command sensed that it was high time Mölders had a rest. At the end of July 1941 he was withdrawn from the front, promoted full colonel and given the appointment of *General der Jagdflieger*, or Inspector of the Luftwaffe Fighter Command. The full weight of the German propaganda machine concentrated on his exploits; he became the first Luftwaffe pilot to receive the coveted Oak Leaves with Swords and Diamonds, and all seemed set for him to rise to the highest ranks as a staff officer. His new staff post in no way turned him into a chairborne warrior; he still flew whenever possible, though not in combat, and visited front-line fighter units to direct air operations and tactics.

In November 1941 he was in the Crimea when he received the stunning news that Ernst Udet, the World War I fighter ace who had risen to the post of Quartermaster-General in charge of Aircraft Supply in Hitler's Germany, had been accidentally shot. That was the official version; what neither Mölders nor his Luftwaffe colleagues knew at this stage was that Udet, disillusioned with the Nazis, had killed himself. The myth of accidental death had to be fostered at all costs, and to this end Udet was to be buried with full military honours in Berlin. Mölders was authorized to fly to Berlin as a member of the Guard of Honour in place of *Reichsmarschall* Hermann Göring, who was 'indisposed'.

In the afternoon of 21 November Mölders boarded a Heinkel 111 bomber at Chaplinka airfield, bound for Germany. During the flight the machine ran into appalling weather and was compelled to land at Lemberg. Conditions were just as bad the next morning, but although the pilot advised Mölders to postpone the flight the ace insisted on an early take-off. At first the trip went reasonably well, despite severe turbulence and heavy rain, but then the Heinkel encountered violent and unexpected headwinds which made nonsense of the navigator's time and fuel calculations. When the engines began to ice up, it was the last straw; the pilot called up the airfield at Breslau and told the controller that he was coming in to land.

Dense cloud covered the field, and the pilot began his approach on instruments. As he broke through the cloud base, he must have seen that he was too low and in danger of undershooting the runway. He crammed on power to go round again—and at the last moment saw a cable railway right in his path. Horrified eyewitnesses saw the bomber rear up as the pilot made a last desperate effort to clear the obstacle. Then the airspeed dropped away, the Heinkel fell ponderously over on one wing and spun into the ground from 400 feet. There were no survivors.

12 Jochen Marseille—
Eagle of the Desert

Captain Eduard Neumann, commanding No. 3 Squadron of *Jagdgeschwader* 27 at Berlin-Doberitz, regarded the newcomer to the unit with some misgivings. It was true that twenty-one-year-old Jochen Marseille had been a fighter pilot since the autumn of 1940, and that his combat record showed that he had shot down eight British fighters in the English Channel area; but it was also true that he was still an Officer Cadet, whereas he should have been promoted to Lieutenant a long time ago.

The reason was not hard to find. It was all there, in his personal file; phrases such as 'showed bravado and played pranks while under training' and 'committed offences in contravention of flying regulations' appeared over and over again. There was even an entry, underlined in red by one furious flight commander, that labelled him a 'flying obscenity'. He could hardly have acquired a worse reputation; all in all, it was a miracle he had not been thrown out of the Luftwaffe. Perhaps thought Neumann, Marseille's ready wit and nonchalant charm—the gifts of a born Berliner—had combined to save his neck.

There was no doubt that the beginnings of Marseille's operational career had been decidedly shaky. His eight victories over the Channel had been achieved only at a cost of six Messerschmitts, for that was the number of times Marseille had been forced to bale out—either as a result of battle damage or engine failure. Even when Neumann's III/JG 27

was transferred to North Africa in April 1941 the young
pilot's bad luck seemed to cling to him; on the flight from
Tripoli to Gazala, the squadron's new base, Marseille's
Messerschmitt 109 developed engine trouble and he was
forced to come down in the desert 500 miles short of his destination.

Underterred, Marseille hitched a ride on an Italian truck,
eventually arriving at a supply depot. He at once reported
to the commanding officer—a General—and passed himself
off as a flight commander, explaining that he had to reach
his base without any delay. The General was by no means
taken in, but he liked Marseille's spirit and obligingly put
his own car—an Opel Admiral—at the young airman's disposal. 'You can repay me by getting fifty victories,' he told
Marseille, who promised to do his best. Neither man
dreamed then that the promise would be fulfilled three
times over. The following day Marseille arrived at Gazala in
style—only a couple of hours after his squadron's Messerschmitts, which had stopped at Benghazi for the night.

Despite his debonair manner, Marseille knew only too
well that his future career depended on his operational record over the next few months, and he determined to prove
that he had the makings of a first-rate fighter pilot. A few
days after III/JG 27 settled in at Gazala he got away to a
good start by shooting down the squadron's first enemy aircraft since its arrival in Africa—a Hurricane, over Tobruk.

His eagerness was almost his undoing; time after time, re-
gardless of personal danger, he dived straight into the middle of a British formation and often returned to base with
his aircraft full of bullet holes. On one occasion, during a
dogfight, he leaned forward in the cockpit—and a burst of
machine-gun fire ripped the back of his helmet. Had it not
been for his sudden movement, the bullets would have shattered his head. In another dogfight over Tobruk his 109 was
badly hit and he had to make a forced landing in no-man's-
land, but he managed to reach the German lines safely. A

few days later his aircraft was hit in the engine and he crash-landed at Gazala, walking unscathed from the wreck.

Eduard Neumann thought it was time to have a word with Marseille. 'You are only alive,' he told him, 'because you have more luck than sense. But don't imagine that it will continue indefinitely. One can overstrain one's luck like one can an aeroplane. You have the makings of a top-notch pilot, but to become one you need time, maturity and experience—certainly more time than you have left if you go on as you have been doing.'

The message sank home, and from now on Marseille devoted much of his time to improving his tactics. He practised shooting from every angle, making dummy attacks on the other aircraft of his squadron, and as the weeks passed his skill increased. During Rommel's summer offensive of 1941 his score grew to eighteen aircraft destroyed and his name was frequently mentioned in dispatches. The high point of this period came on 24 September, when Marseille destroyed five aircraft in a single day. In the morning he destroyed a Martin Maryland bomber, and in the afternoon he shot down four Hurricanes in a fierce half-hour battle between Halfaya Pass and Sidi Barrani. The British fighters tried to form a defensive circle, but the Messerschmitts broke it up and Marseille destroyed his last victim after a hectic chase that led him over Sidi Barrani itself.

In October the rains came, flooding Allied and German airstrips alike and severely curtailing air activity on both sides. At the same time the British launched an autumn offensive, pushing Rommel back to the point from which he had started several months earlier. During this defensive period Marseille's score rose to forty-eight, bringing the award of the Knight's Cross. He was also accorded certain privileges within his squadron; he flew his own 'personal' Messerschmitt, with a large and distinctive yellow 14 painted on its fuselage just aft of the cockpit.

In April 1942 Marseille was promoted First Lieutenant

and given command of III/JG 27; Eduard Neumann was promoted in turn and assumed command of the *Geschwader*. After the defensive battles of the winter months JG 27 was now up to full strength again in both aircraft and pilots and was all set to fly in support of Rommel's renewed spring offensive. Marseille's score continued to mount, and he and his 'Yellow 14' rapidly assumed a legendary quality on both sides of the front. There was plenty of action; in June 1942 Rommel's forces, spearing towards Cairo, were halted at the desert fort of Bir Hacheim, which was gallantly held by the First Free French Brigade under General König, and the sky above it was the scene of fierce air fighting during the nine days before the battered defenders finally capitulated.

On 3 June the Luftwaffe launched a series of heavy Stuka attacks against Bir Hacheim, escorted by JG 27's Messerschmitts. During the first raid of the afternoon the Stukas were intercepted by RAF fighters and the Curtiss P-40s of No. 5 Squadron, South African Air Force, and soon the dive-bombers were beginning to go down in flames. Then Marseille appeared on the scene, together with his wingman, Sergeant Rainer Pöttgen. The two German pilots swept into the middle of the South Africans, who—believing that they were being attacked by a superior force—immediately formed a defensive circle. Marseille got inside it, turning steeply, and gave a P-40 a short burst. The fighter went down vertically and exploded in the desert.

Marseille's tactics were unorthodox. Turning continually inside the circle of enemy fighters, his airspeed low, he kept on firing in short, accurate bursts. A second P-40 went down, followed quickly by a third. In less than twelve minutes the burning wrecks of six South African fighters were scattered over the desert. Circling watchfully over the mêlée, Rainer Pöttgen watched in fascination as one P-40 after another plunged to destruction. Later, he said: 'I had my work cut out counting his victories, noting the times and position, and simultaneously protecting his tail. His judgement of deflection was incredible. Each time he fired I saw his shells strike first the enemy's nose, then travel along to the cockpit. No ammunition was wasted.'

Marseille, in fact, had become a master of low-speed air combat. Supremely confident of his skill in handling a Messerschmitt, of remaining in full control in any attitude and speed range, his usual tactics involved the sacrifice of speed to gain increased manoeuvrability, which enabled him to turn inside an opponent. Once in this position, his excellent deflection shooting did the rest. When he landed after the battle with the South African P-40s, it was found that he had used only ten 20-mm shells and 180 rounds of ammunition in shooting down the six aircraft.

The Germans mounted daily bombing attacks on Bir Hacheim, the North Africa-based Stukas—which suffered heavy losses, despite the efforts of the pilots of Jg 27 and other Luftwaffe fighter units—being reinforced by Junkers 88s from Greece and Crete. Finally, the Germans fixed 10 June as the date for an all-out air and ground assault on the fortress. During the course of the day 250 German bombers carried out three massive raids on Bir Hacheim, dropping 140 tons of bombs, and as the dust and smoke settled the German infantry launched their attack. Meanwhile, high overhead, fierce air battles raged as 168 Messerschmitts joined combat with the P-40s and Hurricanes of the RAF and SAAF—and, for the first time in North Africa, Spitfires. Both sides sustained considerable losses; Marseille destroyed four enemy fighters, bringing his score so far to eighty-one.

Bir Hacheim surrendered on 11 June. Rommel's rear was now secure and his Panzer divisions pushed on rapidly, forcing the Commonwealth troops to retreat towards the Egyptian frontier. The pilots of JG 27 flew intensively during the next three days, and Marseille shot down a further six aircraft. 15 June was a big day, with heavy air fighting over the El Adem sector, and Marseille destroyed four more machines. His score was now ninety-one, and as he approached the magic figure of one hundred the tension among the personnel of JG 27 became almost unbearable, particularly since Marseille had vowed to shoot down his one-hundredth aircraft within the next forty-eight hours. On the morning of 16 June, III/JG 27 carried out two sorties without sighting a single enemy aircraft. A third sortie was flown in the early afternoon, and when the Messerschmitts landed their pilots were jubilant; Marseille had got four more. But there was only a day to go before his self-imposed deadline expired, and even his most ardent admirers wondered if he would achieve his target in time.

They were not kept in suspense for long. The next morning, the whole of JG 27 took off on a fighter sweep. Large numbers of British fighter-bombers were attacking the German ground forces and their supply lines, and there was certain to be action. Shortly after mid-day, excited lookouts sighted Marseille's flight returning to base. A minute later, 'Yellow 14' roared across the airfield at low level, rocking his wings three times. That signified three kills. Then the yellow-marked Messerschmitt made a second run—and once again the wings rocked three times. Six enemy aircraft down in a single sortie—and that brought Marseille's score to 101!

An elated crowd converged on Marseille's fighter as it taxied in. Fellow pilots jumped on the wing, ready to lift the ace from the cockpit and chair him shoulder-high in triumph. But Marseille waved them all away; his face was ashen and he was trembling. He climbed down and lit a cigarette with hands that shook; he was drenched in sweat and seemed hardly able to stand.

His CO, Eduard Neumann, recognized all the classic symptoms of advanced combat fatigue. Taking Marseille by the arm, he led him away through the puzzled and concerned onlookers. When they were alone, Neumann told Marseille bluntly that he was sending him on leave. Marseille protested, but it was no use. The next day he was on board a

Junkers 52, heading out over the Mediterranean for Italy on the first leg of his journey home.

He was away for two months, returning to North Africa on 23 August 1942. During his stay in Germany he had become the nation's idol, as Werner Mölders had been a couple of years earlier. Between Mölders and Marseille, however, there was no similarity other than their prowess as fighter pilots; whereas Mölders had been taciturn, quietly-spoken and paternal, Marseille was the prototype of a twentieth-century knight: dashing, chivalrous, bubbling over with a zest for life and adventure. His leave was one long round of parties; girls flocked to him, and when he returned to North Africa his fan mail was enormous. Dozens of letters arrived addressed simply to the 'Star of Africa'; they always reached their destination.

Even in the desert, Marseille went to great lengths to keep up appearances. His quarters on JG 27's airfield consisted of several tents, linked together to form adjoining rooms which were complete with carpets and furniture. There was even a bar, in which Marseille frequently entertained senior German and Italian officers. The whole was scrupulously cared for by Marseille's faithful batman, a South African negro named Matthias.

When Marseille arrived back in Africa, he found that considerable changes had taken place in the conduct of the desert war. A fierce argument had developed between Rommel and Field Marshal Kesselring, commander of the Luftwaffe in the Mediterranean area. In June Tobruk had fallen to the Germans, and Rommel had declared his intention to push straight on to the Nile Delta and Cairo, giving the British no time to regroup their forces. Kesselring's argument was that such a move would create an enormous logistics problem for the Luftwaffe, whose crews were exhausted and their aircraft badly in need of overhaul. Moreover, the strength of the British Desert Air Force was continuing to grow and the Luftwaffe was in no position to mount attacks on its airfields; this meant that if Rommel persisted in an all-out push towards Cairo there was no guarantee that the Luftwaffe would be able to provide the necessary air support.

Rommel, however, won the argument and the advance went on. The Luftwaffe threw its dwindling resources into the battle, attacking enemy supply depots and troop concentrations. At the end of June JG 27 moved up to Sidi Barrani, and for days on end the fighter pilots flew sortie after sortie with hardly anything in their stomachs; as Kesselring had predicted, the supply organization was beginning to break down and JG's provisions were still well to the rear. There was little fuel and still less food. Rommel's drive finally ground to a halt before El Alamein, and it was at this point that Marseille returned to the battle. For a week he saw little action; then on 1 September Rommel made a last attempt to break through at El Alamein. Fierce air battles developed over the front as the Luftwaffe put every available aircraft into the air in a maximum effort.

For Marseille the day began at 08.28, when he shot down a P-40 Kittyhawk. A second P-40 followed quickly, and ten minutes later he claimed a pair of Spitfires. In an incredible ten minutes between 10.55 and 11.05, while escorting Stukas in a raid on Alem el Halfa, he claimed no fewer than eight Kittyhawks, and in a third sortie between 17.47 and 17.53 he destroyed five more south of Imayid, bringing his total score for the day to an unbelievable seventeen.

Later, this claim was to be the subject of much controversy. It was bitterly contested by the RAF, who stated that Marseille's claim exceeded the total British losses for that day. Yet every one of Marseille's claims on 1 September was confirmed by his wingmen, who noted times and locations, and the possibility of some conspiracy is out of the question. Moreover, the losses of the British and South African fighter squadrons for 1 September, taken together, did in fact exceed the claims of all German fighter pilots by about ten per cent. There the argument must be left, for there is no way of resolving it; but an argument it will doubtless remain as long as there are students of air warfare.

Two days later, Marseille was awarded the Diamonds to the Knight's Cross. He was now the Luftwaffe's most highly-decorated pilot, possessing the Knight's Cross with Oak Leaves and Swords and the Italian Gold Medal for Bravery, which only three men were awarded during World War II.

During September Marseille's score—counting the disputed claim of the 1st—rose to 158 enemy aircraft destroyed. His 158th victim, a Spitfire, almost succeeded in shooting him down; Marseille only gained the advantage and despatched his opponent after a savage dogfight lasting over a quarter of an hour. It was his last victory. On 30 September, together with eight other Messerschmitts of his squadron, he took off to provide top cover for a formation of Stukas. The dive-bombers attacked their targets without incident; no enemy aircraft were sighted and the Messerschmitts turned for home, their job completed.

At 11.35 hours, as the fighter formation cruised at 4,500 feet, Marseille's voice suddenly came over the radio. 'There's smoke in my cockpit—I can't see clearly.' The other pilots saw him open the small ventilation hatch in the side of the canopy, and a streamer of dense smoke poured out. Marseille kept on repeating that he was unable to see, and the others passed directions to him over the R/T. Ground control, who had heard his radio call, advised him to bale out, but the Messerschmitts were still three minutes' flying time away from the German lines and Marseille refused. He had always had a horror of being taken prisoner.

The smoke grew worse. It poured back from the cockpit, engulfing the rear fuselage and tail. The seconds dragged by endlessly. At last, the formation entered friendly territory. Marseille called: 'I've got to get out.'

The others saw his jettisoned canopy whirl away in the slipstream. A second later the dark bundle of Marseille's body fell from the cockpit as he turned the Messerschmitt over on its back. It seemed to strike the tailplane a glancing blow, then dropped away towards the desert.

Horrified, Marseille's fellow pilots saw his body dwindle to a tiny speck, merging with the tawny background of sand and scrub. There was no parachute. They buried him where he fell, and a weeping Matthias placed a few personal trinkets in the grave before the sand closed over the remains of the Eagle of the Desert. Later, in the wake of the Battle of El Alamein, the tanks of Field Marshal Montgomery's victorious Eighth Army rolled past the spot. For Jochen Marseille, the Desert Star had set; for the Afrika Korps, it was already on the wane.

13 Saburo Sakai—Ace of the Rising Sun

The formation of Japanese Navy aircraft droned steadily on over the featureless waters of the Pacific. There were seventeen of them; eight twin-engined Mitsubishi G4M 'Betty' bombers escorted by nine A6M 'Zero' fighters.

An hour earlier on that afternoon of 4 July, 1944, the aircraft had taken off in a cloud of volcanic dust from the bomb-shattered airstrip on the island of Iwo Jima. For two days, American carrier aircraft had struck at the island in overwhelming force, destroying installations and virtually wiping out the Japanese combat squadrons based there. At the end of those two days, the Japanese Navy's complement of eighty Zero fighters had been reduced to nine, while the eight Betty bombers were all that remained of an original wing of fifty machines. What was left of the Japanese Naval Air Arm on Iwo was being pitted against impossible odds. Somewhere ahead of the formation, detected by a reconnaissance aircraft the previous day, lay a large American task force, and Japanese Intelligence guessed that its destination was Iwo Jima. Intelligence, in fact, was only partly correct; although part of the task force had been detailed to bombard Iwo, the bulk of the American ships was destined for the Philippines.

Japanese Naval Air Command had ordered every available aircraft on Iwo Jima to launch an immediate attack on the enemy. When the order first came through there had been plenty of machines to do the job; but then the US car-

rier aircraft had launched three massive strikes on the island. In the last raid alone, forty Zeros had been destroyed
either in the air or on the ground. The survivors were now
on their way to carry out their hopeless mission. The nine
Zeros flew in three 'vics', shepherding the lumbering
bombers. The pilots of fighters and bombers alike knew that
in a very short time they were going to die. Once in the target area they were each to select an enemy ship and dive
into it.

Leading the third 'vic' of Zeros, Ensign Saburo Sakai was
filled with a deep sense of futility. Before sacrificing their
own lives, the Zero pilots had the task of ensuring that the
bombers broke through the enemy defences—and the carriers of the US task force could put up four hundred fighters.
Nine against four hundred was long odds, even for experienced pilots such as Sakai, whose combat career had begun
with operations over Manchuria in the late 1930s.

The formation passed the black, bare rock that was Pagan
Island, their first sight of land since leaving Iwo. Forty minutes later, a line of towering storm clouds rose over the horizon; somewhere beneath them lay the American warships.
The Japanese began a gradual descent from 16,000 to 13,000
feet. The pilots would begin their death-dive as soon as the
warships were sighted, building up speed in the faint hope
of evading the fighters that were sure to be waiting, alerted
by radar.

A minute later, the glitter of sunlight on a polished wing
surface ahead and above caught Sakai's eye. More flashes,
and an avalanche of American fighters came tumbling down
towards the Japanese. They were F6F Hellcats, and there
were at least twenty of them. In line astern they ripped
through the Japanese formation, firing as they went. The
two leading Bettys disintegrated in a cloud of flame and
debris as the torpedoes they carried exploded. Two more
Hellcat formations—more than fifty fighters—converged on
the Japanese. The Zero pilots had orders to avoid combat,

but this was now impossible. Frantically, they turned to face the enemy. A Hellcat flashed through Sakai's sights and he fired; the enemy fighter went into a series of uncontrollable flick rolls and plunged down, trailing smoke.

One by one, as the Zeros fought desperately for their lives, the Bettys were being hacked out of the sky. In less than a minute seven of the bombers were destroyed, their charred remains fluttering down towards the ocean under spreading clouds of black smoke. Two Zeros went down, balls of brilliant flame.

Sakai realized that it was pointless to fight on; the odds were too overwhelming. Gradually, in the middle of a whirling mass of Hellcats, his two wingmen sticking to him like glue, he edged his way towards a large storm cloud. Seizing their chance, the three Zeros dived between two groups of Hellcats and plunged into the sheltering cloud. For endless minutes they fell through swirling darkness, their machines buffeted by the severe turbulence in the heart of the cumulus, eventually dropping from the cloud base a few hundred feet over a sea lashed by torrential rain.

The three fighters re-formed and turned south, still searching for the American ships. The pilots saw nothing but the blinding rain, lashing the sea into a fury and reducing visibility to only a few hundred yards. They flew on for another half hour, with the visibility growing worse all the time and dusk beginning to creep over the sea. In the end Sakai realized the hopelessness of their task; fighting an inner battle against his long years of strict discipline and training, he decided to abandon the mission. The three Zeros turned and set course for Iwo.

Three hours later, they landed in darkness on the island's airstrip. One other Zero pilot had also found his way back, together with the sole surviving Betty bomber. The latter's pilot had found the ships, released his torpedo and run for it, evading the prowling Hellcats by a miracle. He, too, had broken the strict ties of discipline and refused to throw away his life needlessly. The following day, sixteen American warships appeared off Iwo Jima. They were unopposed. Their first salvo blasted the airstrip and wiped out the four Zeros that had fought their way back only a few hours earlier. How different it had been only two short years ago, when Japan was mistress of the Pacific skies!

For Saburo Sakai, the Pacific war had begun on 8 December 1941, a few hours after Japanese carrier aircraft shattered the US Pacific Fleet at Pearl Harbor. Then an NCO pilot in the Imperial Japanese Navy, with two kills to his credit already during action over China, he was a member of a naval air squadron based at Tainan, on Formosa, when orders came through for the first mission against the Americans; forty-five Zeros were to escort fifty-three bombers in an attack on US airfields in the Philippines. The mission involved a round trip of up to 1,200 miles, but the Japanese pilots had developed low-speed cruising tactics that almost doubled the Zero's endurance and the distance itself was no object. The subsequent appearance of Japanese fighters over targets that were theoretically outside their radius of action must have come as an unpleasant surprise to the Americans during those first weeks of the war.

The Japanese arrived over Clark Field, their objective in the Philippines, to find the American aircraft lined up in neat ranks. Sakai's fighter group, some minutes ahead of the bomber formation, circled watchfully overhead; below them, at 15,000 feet, five Curtiss P-40s also circled, but they made no move to intercept the Zeros.

As soon as the bombers appeared, unloading their bombs with amazing precision on Clark Field's runways and installations, Sakai took his section down to strafe the parked aircraft. The Zeros shot up a pair of B-17s, and as they climbed steeply away the P-40s finally decided to attack. Sakai and his two wingmen broke hard, turning to meet the P-40s. The manoeuvre took the Americans by surprise and they scattered in all directions. Four of the P-40s vanished in the pall of smoke that now rose over the airfield; the fifth turned in the opposite direction—straight into Sakai's line of fire. It went down vertically, its cockpit shattered—the first American aircraft to be shot down in the Philippines.

During the next few days the Zeros of the Tainan Wing maintained a continual air umbrella over the Philippines, preventing serious American air interference with the Japanese invasion force that was going ashore in the north of the island group. On 10 December, while circling at 18,000 feet over the convoy, Sakai saw several geysers of water suddenly erupt around the ships; looking round, he saw a lone B-17 Flying Fortress a few thousand feet higher up, heading for safety at full throttle. With nine other Zeros, Sakai caught up with the American bomber. One by one the Japanese fighters made their passes in the face of heavy defensive fire, but despite the weight of bullets it was receiving the B-17 refused to burn. Finally, Sakai and two other pilots closed right in, wingtip to wingtip, and poured fire into the great bomber. Shot to pieces, with rivers of fuel pouring from shattered tanks, it began to go down. Eight of its crew managed to bale out before it crashed just short of Clark Field.

Soon after this incident, Sakai and twenty-six other Zero pilots of the Tainan Wing flew to Jolo airfield in the Sulu Islands to cover the Japanese landings in Borneo. The Japanese ground forces were being severely harassed by B-17s, and there was a promise of considerable action. The Japanese, however, were in for a shock; the American bombers were B-17Fs, fitted with a rear gun turret—unlike the earlier model B-17E shot down over Clark Field—and the first Zero pilots who encountered them made no headway at all, often returning to base with their fighters riddled with .5 bulletholes. Hits with the Zeros' armament seemed to have no effect on the four-engined heavy bombers.

Like the Luftwaffe's fighter pilots later in the war, the Japanese adopted head-on passes against the B-17s; but in these early days of the Pacific war the American bombers were generally flying in loose formation, which enabled the pilots of individual aircraft to take evasive action. On 25 January 1942 Sakai himself came up against one such B-17F formation and spent several minutes attacking one of the aircraft from all angles, braving the storm of machine-gun bullets from the seven other American aircraft. His target finally dropped down into the cloud layer, trailing smoke, and he was credited with a 'probable'. For Sakai and the other Zero pilots, the difficulty experienced in shooting down the Flying Fortresses was a grim foretaste of things to come, when an even mightier generation of American strategic bombers would roam over the skies of the Japanese home islands.

In February 1942 Sakai's wing was switched from the Borneo sector in support of the Japanese invasion of Java. The Zeros quickly established complete air superiority, easily outclassing their opponents—mainly P-36s and Brewster Buffaloes of the Dutch East Indies Air Arm, American P-40s, and a handful of British Hurricanes. By the last day of February, Sakai had increased his personal score to thirteen.

The following month the Tainan Wing moved southwards once again to Bali Island in the wake of the victorious Japanese advance. The Zeros had been there less than a week when orders came through for a fresh move: this time to Rabaul, in New Britain, where the Japanese were building up their forces for an offensive aimed at the complete occupation of New Guinea. Much of the Japanese air effort during this phase was directed against the Allied bastion of Port Moresby, and in order to provide more effective fighter cover for the bombers operating from Rabaul thirty Zeros of the Tainan Wing, including Sakai, were moved to the recently-captured airfield at Lae on the east coast of New Guinea early in April.

Lae was only 180 miles from Port Moresby, and during

the months that followed the sky over the mountainous jungle terrain separating the two bases became the scene of bitter air battles as the Allies threw in all their resources to halt the Japanese advance. For the first time, the Zero squadrons began to sustain real losses in combat with superbly-flown American and Australian fighters, notably P-39 Airacobras and P-40 Tomahawks, although the Japanese still managed to retain their overall superiority; on 23 April, for example, Sakai's squadron engaged six B-26 Marauder bombers, 15 P-40s and P-39s in the Moresby area and claimed the definite destruction of two bombers and six P-40s. The next day, the Zeros shot down six out of seven P-40s and five B-26s on the ground in a strafing attack. Despite the ascendancy of the Zeros, the Allied bomber squadrons continued to press home their attacks on the Japanese bases with great courage, the twin-engined B-26 Marauders and B-25 Mitchells suffering heavy losses in the process. On 24 May the Zeros accounted for five out of six B-25s that bombed Lae, and a loss of this magnitude was by no means an exception.

The Allies, however, continued to pour material into Port Moresby, and although the Japanese fighter pilots failed to realize it as yet the tide of the Pacific War was already beginning to turn against their country. On 5 June, United States warships and aircraft inflicted a crushing defeat on a Japanese naval task force at Midway, sinking four aircraft carriers together with their complement of 280 aircraft and most of their pilots. Without naval supremacy, the Japanese had no hope of sustaining their Pacific offensive; after Midway, the advantage they had gained by their surprise attack on Pearl Harbor was steadily eroded.

Meanwhile, the Allied build-up in Port Moresby went on unchecked, and the air forces of both sides continued to hit one another hard. Port Moresby was proving a tough nut to crack; the Japanese had originally planned a massive amphibious assault on it, but this had to be cancelled when the Allies achieved local naval superiority during the Battle of the Coral Sea in May—the first naval battle in history in which no shot was fired by surface forces, all the action being undertaken by carrier aircraft.

In July, in a desperate final attempt to eradicate Port Moresby, the Japanese landed a division at Buna, one hundred miles south of Lae. The soldiers launched themselves towards their objective through the fearful jungles of the Owen Stanley Mountains—one of the most inhospitable areas in the world, with swamps that could swallow a whole battalion without trace, terrible humidity, every tropical disease known to man and insects that turned every square inch of exposed skin into an inflamed pool of agony. There were to be few survivors of that nightmare expedition. The landing at Buna in itself brought respite to Moresby, for every available Japanese aircraft was called upon to provide continual air cover over the beach-head. There was no respite for the fighter pilots, for the Allied bombers pressed home their attacks in all weathers.

For Saburo Sakai, 22 July was a hectic day—and one full of surprises. During his first sortie of the day, he was circling over the beach-head under a layer of cloud at 7,000 feet when a stick of bombs suddenly erupted among the troops and equipment below. Sakai guessed that one or more Allied aircraft had dropped briefly through the overcast, released their bombs without being seen and climbed quickly back into cloud cover once more.

The guess was correct. A few minutes later, Sakai spotted a tiny speck slipping out of the fringe of the cloud to the south-east, and turned in pursuit with his flight of Zeros. The fighters rapidly closed the distance, and the fleeing aircraft was identified as a twin engined Lockheed Hudson. At 600 yards, confident of an easy kill, Sakai opened fire—and then the unexpected happened. The Hudson suddenly pulled up in a steep climbing turn, rolled out and came roaring head-on at the Zeros, who scattered wildly. The Hudson pilot handled his aircraft like a single-engined fighter, per-

forming a series of brilliant evasive manoeuvres that threw
the Japanese completely off balance while his rear-gunner
loosed off uncomfortably accurate bursts of fire at the pursuers.

For ten minutes the Zero pilots tried every trick in the
book in an effort to nail the elusive bomber, and failed to
score a single hit. Finally, a lucky burst shattered the rear
turret and killed the valiant gunner. Sakai now closed in to
twenty yards and fired a long burst, aiming for the Hudson's
starboard wing. Flames streamed back and the stricken
bomber lost height rapidly until it was skimming the jungle.
Seconds later it crashed, scything a lane through the trees. A
dense cloud of black smoke boiled up from the lake of blazing fuel that marked its grave.

The Zeros formed up and set course for Lae. A few minutes later, they sighted five P-39 Airacobras, flying low over
the sea. Although he and his colleagues were short of fuel
and ammunition Sakai decided to attack, arrowing down towards the American fighters in a steep dive. Sakai picked on
one P-39, which raced towards the Owen Stanley Mountains. At a range of only thirty yards Sakai was preparing to
dispose of the Airacobra with a single well-aimed burst
when the American pilot suddenly baled out at only 150
feet. Miraculously his parachute streamed open just before
he hit the ground in a small clearing, and Sakai saw him
limp towards the shelter of the trees. The Japanese pilot
claimed the P-39 as his forty-ninth victory.

The beach-head patrols continued, and on 26 July Sakai
boosted his score by shooting down two B-26 Marauders
within sight of Port Moresby. Three days later, the course of
events took a new turn when another Japanese fighter
squadron in the area reported a brush with American Navy
Dauntless dive-bombers and F4F Wildcat fighters. These
were grim tidings, for if the Americans had an aircraft carrier to spare for operations off New Guinea it meant that
there must be no truth in Tokyo's claim that the Japanese

had scored a resounding success at Midway. The doubts
that were fast growing in the minds of Sakai and the other
pilots were strengthened when, early in August, there came
the shattering news that the Americans had invaded Guadalcanal Island. It was indeed, thought Sakai, odd behav-
iour for a nation that was supposed to be on the defensive.

On 2 August, however, these gloomy shadows were temporarily dispelled by a resounding success achieved by Sakai's squadron. Circling over Buna at 12,000 feet, the Zero
pilots sighted five B-17 Flying Fortresses approaching the
beach-head at the same height. The day before, Sakai had
managed to shoot down a Fortress after a stiff battle by
means of a head-on attack, and now his fellow pilots were
planning to use the same tactics. The nine Zeros went for
the B-17s in line astern at 500-yard intervals. Each pilot held
his fire until the bomber he had selected filled his sights,
then put a lengthy burst into the nose section before climbing hard over the target.

On the first pass, a Zero's cannon shells ripped into a Fortress's bomb-bay. The B-17 vanished in a mighty explosion;
the Zero sped through the billowing smoke-cloud and rock-
eted up into the sky, apparently undamaged. Sakai attacked
in turn, holding his Zero steady until the bomber's bulk
filled the sky ahead. He squeezed the trigger; nothing happened. He climbed desperately away through a cone of defensive fire, cursing himself. In his excitement he had forgotten to take off the safety-catch. Behind him, another Zero
had completed its attack and a second Fortress was going
down, enveloped in flame. A minute later a third B-17
spiralled earthwards out of control, its pilot and co-pilot
dead in their bullet-shattered cockpit. The two remaining
B-17s split up and Sakai went after one of them, attacking
from below and watching his shells churn up the bomber's
port wing. An instant later, his fighter shot through an inferno of smoke and flame as the bomber blew up.

Sakai emerged into clear sky, his ears ringing from the

concussion of the explosion, and looked round in time to see three Airacobras approaching from the east, bearing down on the eight other Zeros who were intent on butchering the sole surviving B-17. Sakai turned and got behind the P-39s, whose pilots had not seen him, and attacked the rearmost aircraft. One of the Airacobra's wings tore away and the fighter spiralled down, shedding fragments. The other Zeros now turned hard to meet the two remaining P-39s and destroyed both of them within seconds.

Meanwhile, Sakai went after the B-17, which—although badly hit—was limping steadily towards safety. The bomber's gunners were still firing, and bullets ripped into the Zero. Sakai made one pass, then his colleagues returned from the battle with the P-39s to finish the job. Shot to pieces, the B-17 went down over the coast. The American gunners, however, had had the last word. A Zero broke away, trailing a thin streamer of white smoke, and disappeared over the jungle. It was never seen again.

A few days later the Americans launched their invasion of Guadalcanal, and the Zeros were recalled to Rabaul to fly escort missions for bombers attacking the enemy beach-head—a task that involved a round trip of 1,100 miles on every sortie. Almost as soon as the Zeros of Sakai's squadron arrived back at Rabaul, they were refuelled and rearmed and ordered to accompany twenty-seven Betty bombers to the island. The outward flight was peaceful, the formation droning over a brilliantly blue sea. Sakai noticed a particularly beautiful island, bright green and shaped like a horseshoe, and looked for it on his map—a simple action that was later to save his life. The formation arrived over the American beach-head, and the bombers began their run towards the armada of enemy ships clustered offshore. Overhead, the Zeros were soon battling desperately with shoals of Grumman Wildcats—the first aircraft of this type Sakai had seen. He shot down one Wildcat, then was himself attacked by a Douglas Dauntless dive-bomber. The Dauntless overshot and he followed it down through a thin layer of cloud, raking it with cannon shells. The bomber fell away, out of control, and the pilot baled out.

Climbing back up to 13,000 feet, Sakai spotted what appeared to be a tight formation of eight Wildcats some distance ahead, and went after them. Just as he was about to open fire he realized his mistake: the machines were Grumman Avenger torpedo-bombers—and a total of sixteen rearward-firing guns was pointing at him. Sakai pressed the trigger, and at that same instant the Americans opened fire too. Sakai felt a violent blow tear at his body, the world dissolved in a blinding red flash and he passed out.

It was the wind howling through the shattered cockpit canopy that brought him round. The Zero was plunging towards the sea. Instinctively, Sakai pulled back the stick and felt the pressure as the fighter came out of its dive. He could see nothing except a red mist, but the wind force had abated and this told him that he must be approximately in level flight. Tears began to stream from his eyes, washing away the blood that was caked on his cheeks; he began to see again, although everything was just a blur.

The Zero raced across the water, past the dim outlines of American ships that blazed away with everything they had. Once out of range, Sakai eased back the stick and headed in what he hoped was the direction of Rabaul. His senses were gradually returning, and he was able to take stock of his injuries. A bullet had ripped across the top of his head, laying the skull bare. His left side seemed to be completely paralysed and he was blind in his right eye, which was causing fearful pain. All in all, his chances of reaching Rabaul seemed slender indeed; but Sakai was determined not to give up easily. With considerable difficulty he improvised a bandage for his head wound out of his silk scarf and flew on, resisting an overwhelming desire to go to sleep. Once, terrible despair gripped him and he turned back towards Guadalcanal, intent on finding an enemy ship and diving into it.

Then he became rational once more and resumed his original course. He had no real idea of his position and his fighter wandered all over the sky; on one occasion, when he emerged from a period of drowsiness, he found that he was heading in the wrong direction entirely—all of which consumed vital fuel. Shortly after this, the Zero's engine went dead; the fuel in one tank was exhausted and he had to transfer to the other tank by turning a fuel cock on the left of the cockpit. But his left arm was paralysed, and it was only with a superhuman effort that he managed to reach the cock with his right.

He now had sufficient fuel for two hours' flying. In those two hours he had to find a Japanese-occupied island—or die. And he was still flying purely by instinct on a course that might take him to Rabaul—or to a lonely death far out in the ocean.

Thirty minutes went by; an hour. Suddenly, he saw a distant speck on the horizon. As he came closer, it resolved itself into a shape that stirred a chord in his fogged memory. It was the green, horseshoe-shaped island he had passed earlier on his way to Guadalcanal. Fresh hope surged up inside him; he was only sixty miles from Rabaul. Forty-five minutes later, with only a few pints of fuel left in his tank, he made an erratic but safe arrival on Rabaul's familiar airstrip. He taxied in and switched off the engine. Then, and only then, did he collapse into oblivion.

Sakai's wounds kept him in hospital until the end of January 1943. On his discharge he reported to his old unit, the Tainan Fighter Wing, which was now based in Japan, and received promotion to Warrant Officer. In March 1943 the Wing was ordered to return to Rabaul, but Sakai had not regained the sight of his right eye and the senior medical officer would not pass him fit for operational flying. The Wing arrived at Rabaul on 3 April, without Sakai. Later, he learned of the disaster that overwhelmed it; in just four missions, 49 Zeros were shot out of the sky. Of the 150 pilots who had been with the Wing when Sakai joined it in 1941, only a dozen or so were now left.

In April 1944, after a year spent as a flying instructor, Sakai at last won his fight with the medical authorities and was re-assigned to an operational unit—the Yokosuka Air Wing. Soon afterwards the unit left for Iwo Jima, and in the weeks that followed Sakai finally realized the full magnitude of the disaster that was rapidly engulfing Japan. The American task forces, with all their awesome striking power, were roaming the Pacific almost at will, and the dwindling Japanese air squadrons were being relentlessly hunted to destruction by the swarms of carrier based fighters. The Japanese aces who had spearheaded the air offensive in the Pacific two years earlier were gone, scattered over the ocean with the charred cinders of their aircraft.

Sakai returned to Japan from Iwo at the end of July 1944, with the handful of survivors of the Yokosuka Wing. To their amazement, the Americans had not invaded the devastated island. It would be another eight months before they launched their invasion, by which time the Japanese had turned Iwo into a bastion.

Sakai spent the next few months as a test pilot, flying a variety of new fighter aircraft designed to replace the ageing Zeros that still equipped the majority of first-line squadrons in the Pacific. In January 1945 he was assigned to a new unit, the Matsuyama Fighter Wing, which was equipped with machines of the type he had recently tested: the Kawanishi N1K Shiden (Violet Lightning), known to the Allies as 'George'. The Shiden, armed with four cannon, was one of the finest fighter aircraft ever designed by the Japanese—but it had come too late. In the spring of 1945 Japan's aircraft factories were being pounded by the mighty B-29 bombers of the US Twentieth Air Force, and the Japanese fighter airfields themselves were subjected to attacks in growing strength by the swarms of Hellcats and Corsairs operating from task forces that roved unopposed off the coasts of the home islands.

The end came quickly now. In the summer of 1945 Sakai, who had not flown operationally with the Matsuyama Wing, was posted back to the Yokosuka Wing; this unit was now equipped with Mitsubishi J2M Raiden (Thunderbolt) fighters, which had enjoyed some success against the B-29s. Then the Americans began to escort their bombers with P-51 Mustangs, and it was the Raiden's turn to suffer; although fast and well-armed, it lacked the manoeuvrability of the American fighter.

On 13 August, Sakai and the other pilots were assembled and told the shattering news that Japan, in the wake of the atomic bombs on Hiroshima and Nagasaki, had decided to accept the Allied surrender terms. All operational flying was to cease. Stunned and broken, the pilots wandered aimlessly about the base. Sakai leaned by his aircraft, wanting only to be alone. After a while he was joined by his close friend, Ensign Jiro Kawachi. A few words passed between the two; a pact was made. They would make one last flight together.

That night, the B-29s were over in strength. Two Japanese fighters took off to intercept them: one flown by Sakai, the other by Kawachi. As they climbed away, eight other fighters formed up alongside them in the moonlight; they were not the only pilots who had decided to disobey orders. At 10,000 feet over Tokyo Bay they found a lone B-29 and chased it far out to sea, pressing home attack after attack, heedless of the defensive fire that streamed back towards them. Fifty miles off shore the great bomber began to lose height, finally ditching in a splash of white foam.

The fighters formed up and set course for their base. Far ahead of them, a pinkish glow suffused the sky; the B-29s had completed their crucifixion of Japan's cities.

14 Ivan Kozhedub— Russia's Top Scorer

For the Soviet Union, the first months of 1943 marked the turn of the tide in the battle against the invading Germans. In January, while the steel ring closed relentlessly around von Paulus's trapped Sixth Army at Stalingrad, the Russians launched a major offensive on the Caucasus front, beginning a massive battle that was to last seven weeks.

Now, for the first time since the German invasion in June 1941, the Soviet Air Force was starting to wrest air superiority from the Luftwaffe. Under the guidance of talented pilots such as Alexander Pokryshkin—the Red Air Force's greatest tactician, with a score of German aircraft already to his credit at the end of 1942—the Russian airmen were inflicting growing losses on the enemy.

With the coming of the spring thaw the bitter fighting died down as both sides gathered their strength for the great test that was to come during the following months. The Germans knew with grim certainty that if they lost the initiative now, the way would be open for the Russian steamroller to drive across Europe to the frontiers of Germany.

The greatest trial of strength was bound to take place on the Soviet central front, where two German salients at Orel and Kharkov flanked a deep bulge to the west of Kursk. If the Germans could fight their way through the Russian defences north and south of Kursk they would split the Soviet front in two and inflict a shattering defeat on the Red Army.

In this critical sector the Germans had concentrated seventy divisions and nearly a million men, against which the Russians had twelve field armies, including two crack Guards Armies. They also moved up the biggest concentration of air power seen on the Eastern Front so far; five Air Armies, numbering over 2,000 aircraft.

In March 1943, while the build-up continued, a young twenty-three-year-old fighter pilot joined his squadron on the Kursk front. His name was Ivan Nikitievitch Kozhedub, and he had yet to come to grips with the enemy. He was a very ordinary man: the son of a poor peasant, born in the Ukrainian village of Obrasheyevka. His father wanted him to become an engineer, but it was not long before he began to realize that his son cherished other ambitions. For Ivan had a secret dream. One day, a schoolteacher had said to him: 'Choose as your inspiration a man who has done well, and follow his example all your life.' The boy did not have to search far for his inspiration: it lay in the exploits of a famous Soviet airman, Valery Shkalov, who had flown over the North Pole to the USA in 1937. Ivan knew exactly what he wanted out of life; with a kind of desperation, he wanted to fly.

Ivan, however, loved his father. The last thing he wanted was to hurt the old man, who had made so many sacrifices for him. So he studied hard, and although he was not a brilliant pupil he gained entry to a technical college. At this time—the late 1930s—the Soviet aviation industry was expanding in leaps and bounds, and the Komsomol, the Soviet youth organization of which Kozhedub was a member, was actively encouraging young people of both sexes to learn to fly. To this end a rash of state-sponsored flying clubs sprang up all over the USSR, and in 1939 Ivan joined one at Shostka, together with several of his friends. For the time being he kept his membership of the flying club a secret from his father, who he felt might worry in case he was neglecting his studies.

Early in 1940, the secret was out. With a pilot's licence in his pocket, Kozhedub announced that he intended to join the Red Air Force. He was quickly accepted for flying training, and in February 1941 he graduated from his course with an 'above average' pass. His very prowess, in fact, was his undoing; he proved to be such an excellent pilot that instead of being transferred to a front-line squadron he was retained as a flying instructor. He spent the first year of the war in Russia at a training school, suffering the frustration of seeing his students posted one after the other to combat units. It was only in November 1942 that his repeated applications for a transfer bore fruit, and he was able to report to a Fighter Operational Conversion Unit near Moscow.

The unit was equipped with the new Lavochkin La-5 radial-engined fighter, an aircraft which at last enabled the Russians to meet the German Focke-Wulf 190 on equal terms. Kozhedub's instructor was a Major Soldatyenko, who had fought in the Spanish Civil War; the air fighting lessons he passed on to the young pilot were later to prove invaluable.

In March 1943, a newly-promoted Lieutenant, Kozhedub took off from his squadron's airfield near Kursk on his first combat sortie. It was very nearly his last. Half an hour after take-off, having lost contact with his leader, he sighted a formation of enemy aircraft—Messerschmitts—a few thousand feet below him. Single-handed, he dived through the enemy formation, which broke in all directions. Two Messerschmitts went after him and he felt cannon-shell splinters slamming into the armour plating of his seat. Diving away, he raced for base at low level. As he did so the Russian flak opened up and a shell ripped away one of his wingtips. He managed to land safely, but he was conscious that it was hardly an impressive start to his combat career.

On 5 July 1943, Kozhedub and his fellow pilots were awakened by the sound of artillery fire. A few minutes later, they were assembled and addressed by their co, who told them that the battle for the Kursk salient had begun. He also told them that the squadron would not see any action that day, but would be held in reserve. All that day the pilots waited, chafing in frustration as reports came in of great air battles raging over the front line. It was not until the following morning that their chance finally came, when they were briefed to carry out an offensive 'sweep' at dawn. Led by Captain Semyenov, the squadron's twelve La-5s cruised over the battlefield at 10,000 feet, and for the first time the pilots got a first-hand view of the bitter conflict that raged below. Burning tanks and trucks were scattered everywhere, their smoke trailing over the countryside in a great banner. Even at this height the acrid smell penetrated the Lavochkins' cockpits, making the pilots' eyes stream.

Suddenly, they saw the enemy—twenty Junkers 87 Stukas, crossing the front line with a strong escort of Messerschmitts. The Russian squadron went into a long, shallow dive out of the sun and the Germans failed to see the danger until it was too late. Semyenov's guns hammered and a Stuka went down in flames, one wing torn off by cannon-shells.

Then it was Kozhedub's turn. Shadowed by his wingman, Vassily Mukhin, he closed in on a Stuka and opened fire. He could see his shells sparkling on the enemy aircraft's drab camouflage, but the Stuka stubbornly refused to burn. Koz-hedub poured round after round into it and at last a thin trail of smoke streamed back from its engine cowling. The end came suddenly; the Stuka exploded and cartwheeled over the ground, shedding blazing fragments. An instant later a dark shadow swept over Kozhedub's cockpit. It was a Messerschmitt, driven off in the nick of time by the faithful Mukhin. Sweating, Kozhedub turned away, making a mental note to look behind him in future.

The Russian attack had completely dislocated the German formation and now the Stukas were running for home, leaving several of their number burning on the ground. A minute later the Russians sighted another enemy formation, but while the others went in to the attack Kozhedub, out of ammunition, was forced to return to base with Mukhin.

The following morning Kozhedub destroyed his second Junkers 87, and 24 hours later he added two Messerschmitt 109s to his score. His part in the Battle of Kursk later earned him the award of the Order of the Red Banner, and he was promoted to command his own fighter squadron.

Both on the ground and in the air, Kozhedub and Vassily Mukhin were inseparable. Kozhedub later wrote: 'On the ground Mukhin followed me everywhere, getting used to my every movement. I sometimes forgot he was there, but when I turned round there he would be, hard on my heels. We got to know one another's background, talking for hours on end about our families and our native villages. We slept side by side, ate side by side. And so we formed a first class team based on complete trust: it was to save our lives many times over.'

During the last week of September 1943, Kozhedub's squadron was moved up to occupy an airstrip on the left bank of the River Dnieper. The Germans were holding the opposite bank, but the Russians had managed to establish a bridgehead there. This was to be the scene of some bitter air fighting, and in ten days Kozhedub shot down eleven enemy aircraft. On one occasion, however, he came close to losing his own life.

It happened on 12 October, a day in which he flew several sorties and added two more German aircraft to his score. By the end of the afternoon he and his pilots were exhausted, but nevertheless they took off yet again to fly top cover for Russian reinforcements who were crossing the river. On reaching the combat area they immediately sighted a dozen Stukas and engaged them. The bomber selected by Kozhedub as his target tried to escape by means of a long dive, and the Russian pilot followed it. After a long burst the Stuka went down in flames—but not before the enemy

gunner, fighting to the last, had scored several hits on Kozhedub's fighter. As Kozhedub climbed away, a long ribbon
of flame suddenly burst from the fuel tank in his starboard
wing. The pilot unfastened his straps and was on the point
of baling out when he realized that the fight had carried him
ten miles inside enemy territory. Desperately he sideslipped,
hoping that the slipstream would put out the flames, but the
fire raged as furiously as before.

What now? To be captured by the Germans was unthink-
able. He remembered the case of Captain Gastello, a Russian bomber pilot who—in the early days of the war—had de-
liberately crashed his burning aircraft on to an enemy
armoured column. Grimly, Kozhedub looked around for a
target, determined that if he had to die he would at least
take a few of the enemy with him. Some distance ahead he
spotted a German flak battery. Lining it up in his sights he
plunged towards it in a long, screaming power-dive. The
German gunners scattered in all directions as the burning
Russian fighter streaked towards them. Then the miracle
happened: the fire in the Lavochkin's wing abruptly went
out. At the very last second Kozhedub eased back the stick
and the fighter cleared the gun emplacement by inches.
Staying right 'on the deck' Kozhedub raced for the safety of
the river, pursued by a web of enemy shells. He reached
base without further incident.

By the end of January 1944 Kozhedub's score stood at
twenty-six enemy aircraft destroyed and the Russian propaganda machine was making much of his exploits. In February, his achievements were recognized by the award of Russia's highest decoration: the gold star of the Hero of the
Soviet Union. Shortly afterwards, Kozhedub's squadron was
transferred to Moldavia. The Red Army had gained a foot-
hold in Rumania and the Germans were planning a major
counter-offensive in the Yassy area, supported by considerable numbers of bombers and fighter-bombers.

For several days, from dawn to dusk, the sky reverberated

to the thunder of engines as the opposing air forces struggled for supremacy in the Rumanian sky. Kozhedub increased his personal score by six. In May 1944, Kozhedub received a brand-new 'personal' La-5—a gift from the workers on a collective farm near Stalingrad. At this time, industrial and collective workers all over Russia were devoting their savings to the purchase of new aircraft to be presented to individuals or squadrons of their choice.

Flying this new machine at the head of his squadron, Kozhedub destroyed a further eight enemy aircraft over Rumania in the space of a week. His pilots were operating to the point of exhaustion, for the Luftwaffe was throwing all its available reserves against the advancing Russian ground forces and there was no shortage of 'trade'. One of the fiercest air battles was fought on 15 May, when Kozhedub was leading a dozen fighters on an offensive sweep over the front line. The Russians had not been on patrol for long when they sighted thirty Stukas, escorted by eight Messerschmitts, and swept down to the attack. Two Stukas were quickly shot down and the remainder, scattered all over the sky, released their bombs at random and flew away westwards.

The Russian pilots were climbing away to re-form when they spotted a second large enemy formation. Leaving part of his squadron to deal with the German fighter escort Kozhedub took the rest down in a long, curving dive that brought them behind the bombers. This time the Germans pressed on with considerable determination, and the Russian pilots were soon fighting for their lives as more Messerschmitts came sweeping over the horizon. Kozhedub knocked down a Junkers, then found himself isolated in the middle of a whirling mass of aircraft—all of them German. There was no other Russian fighter in sight; he was completely alone in a sky filled with black crosses. Taking advantage of the Lavochkin's superior rate of climb he zoomed upwards, heading for the shelter of a small cloud. Once he was certain that he had shaken off his pursuers, he levelled out and made a determined effort to pull himself together. His hands were shaking and he was bathed in sweat; fatigue and nervous tension were at last beginning to take their toll.

Looking down, he saw yet another enemy formation crossing the lines. A moment later, the voice of the forward air controller—the Air Force liaison officer attached to the leading army units at the front, who was responsible for directing Russian aircraft in support of the ground forces—came over the radio, using the fighters' callsign. 'Falcons, Falcons! Large group of enemy bombers approaching our positions. Shoot down the leader. I repeat, shoot down the leader!'

This was good sense: the enemy dive-bomber pilots took their timing from the leading aircraft during a formation attack, and if the leader were destroyed it would rob the assault of its co-ordination. Kozhedub acknowledged briefly. There was still no other Russian fighter in sight, and he was now faced with the formidable prospect of taking on a formation of forty enemy aircraft single-handed. A quick glance at his altimeter showed him that he was at 11,000 feet, several thousand feet higher than the enemy. The sun was at his back, and he was dodging in and out of the scant cloud cover. If he could maintain an element of surprise right up to the last moment, he might just get away with it.

He pushed the stick forward and arrowed down towards the German formation. With the combined effects of gravity and the Lavochkin's big Shvetsov radial engine, the acceleration in the dive was fantastic: the leading Stuka leaped up to meet him with frightening speed. The enemy had seen him now and clusters of tracer fanned towards him. There was no time for evasive action. His target filled the whole of his sights and he fired, seeing pieces break away from the Stuka's wings. A slight backward pressure on the stick and the enemy aircraft flashed underneath him, starting to burn. Stukas scattered in all directions as he ripped through their midst; a storm of machine-gun fire followed him as he racked the Lavochkin up in a steep, climbing turn, heading for friendly territory. More tracer flashed past his cockpit and he glanced behind; three Messerschmitts were sitting on his tail. Weaving violently he sped over the Russian lines and the enemy fighters broke away as Russian anti-aircraft fire began to come up. Fifteen minutes later Kozhedub landed safely at his base, utterly exhausted and with only a trickle of fuel left in his tanks. The others were already back —all except three, who had fallen victim to the Messerschmitts.

The relentless Russian drive across Europe continued. In May 1944 the Crimea was liberated, and in June—three years to the day after the Germans had set foot on Russian soil—the Red Army launched a massive offensive aimed at the destruction of Field Marshal Model's Army Group Centre, comprising fifty divisions and nearly one and a quarter million men. The Germans fought back hard, inflicting fearful casualties on the Russians, but by the middle of July Army Group Centre had practically ceased to exist as a cohesive fighting force, and by the end of August the Russians had battered their way to the borders of East Prussia. In September they occupied Rumania and Bulgaria, sweeping into Yugoslavia to take Belgrade and then swinging north-west into Hungary. By mid-December, the front line stretched from Yugoslavia to the Baltic, slicing through Poland and Czechoslovakia and running along the East Prussian frontier.

Behind this vast front, for the final drive into the heart of Germany, the Russians assembled five million men, backed up by 17,000 combat aircraft. The Luftwaffe was outnumbered by ten to one, but on the airfields dotted among the eight defensive lines between the River Oder and Berlin the Germans had assembled some of their finest combat units. Pilots like Kozhedub, who had battled their way to Germany in the wake of the Russian advance, knew with a grim certainty that some of the bloodiest fighting was yet to come.

For Ivan Kozhedub, the last phase of the air war began in February 1945, when he returned to the front after a brief spell of leave. He was now a full Colonel, three times a Hero of the Soviet Union, and had fifty-five enemy aircraft to his credit—three more than his closest rival, Alexander Pokryshkin. His fighter unit was now equipped with Lavochkin La-7s, improved versions of the La-5 with which Kozhedub had scored his earlier victories.

When Kozhedub returned to action, the Luftwaffe was making determined efforts to wipe out a bridgehead established by the Russians on the west bank of the Oder. These attacks were mostly carried out by Focke-Wulf 190 fighter-bombers, which came in low and fast, dropped their bombs and then zoomed up into cloud cover before the Russians had a chance to react. To combat this menace, the Russians maintained a continual air umbrella over the bridgehead in the hope of catching the elusive 190s.

On 12 February 1945 Kozhedub, with Lieutenant Gromakovsky as his wingman, was leading three pairs of fighters on a defensive patrol over the Russian positions when thirty bomb-carrying Focke-Wulfs dropped out of the clouds ahead like a shoal of fish. Kozhedub and Gromakovsky immediately attacked, at the same time calling up the other two pairs of Russian fighters which had been quartering the sky some distance away. Kozhedub and his wingman each accounted for a Focke-Wulf before breaking away as the second pair of Lavochkins made their attack. Another 190 went down, then the third pair of Russian pilots arrived and attacked in turn. The leader of this pair, Captain Orlov, destroyed a Focke-Wulf but was himself shot down a few seconds later by another enemy fighter. The remaining Focke-Wulfs climbed flat out for the shelter of the clouds with the Russian fighters in pursuit. Kozhedub got the rearmost aircraft in his sights and loosed off a burst at extreme range. It was a lucky shot: the Focke-Wulf hung for a moment, its propeller churning the air, then it flicked on to its back and dived into the ground. It was Kozhedub's fifty-seventh victim.

Three days later, Kozhedub was carrying out a lone armed reconnaissance over the front when he spotted a flicker of movement against the snow-covered ground. Diving down to investigate, he found himself a few hundred yards behind a type of aircraft he had never encountered before: a Messerschmitt 262 jet. At full throttle the Russian fighter closed in rapidly; the 262 pilot spotted the danger and streams of black smoke poured from his twin turbines as he crammed on power, but it was too late. Torn apart by a stream of cannon-shells, the sleek jet fighter scythed into a wood and exploded.

At dawn on 16 April 1945, the Russians launched their great offensive across the Oder. Russian fighters were now ranging freely over the sky of Berlin, and it was here that Kozhedub—having added two more enemy aircraft to his score in March—chalked up his last pair of victories in the evening of 17 April. He was carrying out a patrol with a new wingman, Dmitri Titorenko, over the north-west suburbs of the German capital when he sighted a mixed formation of about forty Focke-Wulfs and Messerschmitts fleeting through the curtain of dusk and smoke that hung over the dying city. Climbing hard, the Russians took advantage of some scattered cloud a few thousand feet higher up, using it as cover as they shadowed the enemy.

Kozhedub decided to take a risk. It was two against forty, but height and speed were in the Russians' favour and the sun was behind them. He gave a curt order to his wingman and the two Lavochkins hurtled down on the rearmost echelon of enemy fighter-bombers, holding their fire until they were within almost point-blank range. Kozhedub loosed off a short burst and a Focke-Wulf disintegrated; a second swung into his line of fire and bits fell off it as his shells struck home, but it flicked out of trouble. A third Focke-Wulf, Titorenko's victim, went down vertically into the ruined streets of Berlin.

The enemy formation broke in all directions, doubtless believing that they were being attacked by a large number of Russian fighters. Most of the enemy turned westwards, jettisoning their bombs; one, however, went into a long dive at maximum speed towards the Russian lines. Kozhedub followed him, coming within range just as the Focke-Wulf pilot released his bomb on some unseen target. It was his last act: an instant later Kozhedub's shells ripped off his port wing and the Focke-Wulf flicked into a series of vicious rolls that ended when it hit the ground. It was Kozhedub's sixty-second, and last, victim. The end came rapidly now; by 25 April the Russians had Berlin completely encircled in a ring of fire and steel, and the final collapse of the capital was only a matter of days away. Kozhedub himself was not there to witness the final surrender, having flown to Moscow to represent the Soviet Air Force at the traditional May Day Parade.

During his wartime career, Ivan Kozhedub had made 330 operational sorties and had taken part in 120 air combats. He was never wounded or shot down. After the war he was twice elected to the USSR Parliament, and in 1950 he was promoted to the rank of Guards Major General at the age of thirty—the youngest General in Soviet military history.